KT-484-146

THE gastropub COOKBOOK

ANOTHER HELPING

MITCHELL BEAZLEY

THE gastropub COOKBOOK
ANOTHER HELPING

Diana Henry

photographs by Simon Wheeler

For all the gastropub chefs who have given me recipes and fed me wonderful food, both for this book and the last one. You're a load of mad eejits but you do a great job...

The Gastropub Cookbook – Another Helping
by Diana Henry

First published in Great Britain in 2008
by Mitchell Beazley,
an imprint of Octopus Publishing Group Limited,
2–4 Heron Quays, London E14 4JP
An Hachette Livre UK Company
www.octopusbooks.co.uk

© Octopus Publishing Group Limited 2008
Text © Diana Henry 2008
Photographs © Simon Wheeler 2008
All rights reserved. No part of this publication may be reproduced or utilized in any form by any means, electronic or mechanical, including photocopying, recording or by any information storage and retrieval system, without prior written permission of the publishers.

A CIP catalogue record for this book is available from the British Library.

ISBN 978-1-84533-337-9

While all reasonable care has been taken during the preparation of this edition, neither the publisher, editors, nor the authors can accept responsibility for any consequences arising from the use thereof or from the information contained therein.

Commissioning Editor: Becca Spry
Art Director: Tim Foster
Deputy Art Director: Yasia Williams-Leedham
Photographer: Simon Wheeler
Designer: Miranda Harvey
Project Editor: Ruth Patrick
Editor: Hattie Ellis
Proofreader: Marion Moisy
Production: Lucy Carter
Index: Helen Snaith

Typeset in Baskerville
Colour reproduction by Sang Choy, Singapore
Printed and bound by Toppan, China

contents

introduction

It's now over 15 years since David Eyre and Mike Belben set the gastropub ball rolling by opening The Eagle in London's Farringdon Road. These days there's a gastropub on practically every corner. Gastropubs get their own section in eating out guides and there are several annual guidebooks entirely devoted to them.

But there has been, as with all trends, a backlash. The reason is understandable. In the wake of the success of The Eagle, big business got in on the gastropub trend. Think how many chain pubs now imitate some of the characteristics of the original gastropubs, rolling them out in kit form. These pubs are what gastropubs were an antidote to: blandness and crass commercialism. Some breweries, recognising a good way to make money, now send out information packs to landlords telling them how to turn their pub into a gastropub. There are also smaller businesses with as many as eight gastropubs in their portfolio, all fairly similar in style, run according to a formula, and one well-known hotel group is planning to open 75 gastropubs in the next 18 months.

Famous chefs who are well known for high-end dining have got in on the act as well. And since some don't want to be at the pub stoves themselves, you're forced to conclude that they might be doing it for the money. And that's never going to produce a truly individual place. (Heston Blumenthal, incidentally, is one mega-chef who is not doing this – his pub, The Hind's Head in Bray – is exemplary and he has clearly established it as an enriching adjunct to The Fat Duck.).

There have been endless articles lamenting the demise of the British boozer, ('I've Got Gastrophobia' or 'The Curse of the Chilli Grilled Squid') and giving advice on how to recognise a fake gastropub (for example, that the bad ones have menus painted on their blackboards rather than written in chalk, because the food is never going to change). And the countryside is dotted with pubs that have been refurbished with acres of tongue and groove and painted in Farrow and Ball only to offer unremarkable food in characterless surroundings. Of course there are bad dining pubs. There is a weight of bad restaurants and cafes in this country, too, but nobody thinks we should get rid of restaurants or cafes as a genre.

So now I'll tell you all the good – even the great – things about gastropubs. And I'll start with a chef, Emily Watkins, of the estimable Kingham Plough: 'Gastropub, sadly, came to mean a place that could turn out just about passable Thai fishcakes,' she said to me. 'But that is changing. We are now in the throes of reinventing the British pub. They offer good ales, wines and modern British food, and support local producers and farmers. And that is certainly the kind of place I want to cook in and to be in. I love them.' And she's right. Everywhere I went while researching this book I found market gardeners, foragers and small breweries now thriving because they were supplying a good local gastropub. Just think: as the supermarkets exploit and undervalue these people, gastropubs are doing the opposite.

Here's more good news: at a time when pubs close at a rate of up to 27 a week, some are also being rescued and reopened as dining pubs with a new lease of life. Isn't it better to have dining pubs opening rather than drinking pubs disappearing? And what is this nostalgia for the old boozers? I would never want good drinking pubs to disappear. The complete gastro-pubification of Britain would be awful. But many of the pubs now being snapped up and transformed were as dead as a dodo. Banquettes stiff with years of dirt and grease, a couple of amusement arcade games shoved in the corner and filthy loos…who the hell liked these places, except for inveterate alcoholics?

It isn't just that good dining pubs offer a service – great places to eat – but that their existence is beginning to have an effect on restaurant kitchens too. The flow of talented young chefs leaving smart urban restaurants to run a pub continues unabated. It is still the cheapest way to do your own thing. But these chefs don't just want to do a different, more robust kind of cooking; they also want to work in a different way. Paul Adams, the young chef at The Carpenter's Arms in West London explains it: 'I do not want to spend the rest of my life working on a section in a kitchen where I craft six perfect starters,' he says. 'I want to be able to do everything in a kitchen – bread, ice-cream, fish dishes and salads. And I want everyone in my kitchen to do that too. I want to be a cook, not just be a technician.' This is something I kept hearing on my travels.

If he ever returns to a restaurant kitchen, Paul Adams wants to cook the same way he has been cooking in a pub. He wants a kitchen where everyone can do everything. So perhaps eventually gastropubs will have an impact on the way restaurant kitchens function. These young chefs believe their preferred way of operating is the result of working for men who are cooks before they are chefs – men who love real food. An astonishing number of those now running their own dining pubs pay homage to Alastair Little, Simon Hopkinson, Rowley Leigh and Bristol's Stephen Marwick. We owe these men a debt – their reach in our current dining culture is much greater than they realise.

Another question chewed over *ad nauseam* by journalists is how you define a gastropub. Mike Belben, the co-founder of The Eagle, buries his head in his hands at the dining pubs that put linen cloths on the tables. Steve Harris, chef owner of the Michelin-starred Sportsman in Seasalter in Kent, on the other hand, just rolls his eyes heavenwards. 'Do you know the great thing about these places?' he asks. 'They can be whatever you want them to be. For a chef it's

your baby, it's your stage. If you want to turn out complex food, you can, if you want to offer steak sarnies dripping with garlic butter, you can. I couldn't care less what the definition is because the key thing about them is that they give freedom to enthusiastic cooks.'

In the end I went on gut feeling when making my selection for this book. But I have a few markers. In a gastropub you should not be obliged to eat. If all you want is a pint, that's fine. And if you do eat, you should be able to order a bowl of soup without attracting sniffy glances. You should not be served a foam. If I see a foam or a 'cappuccino' of this or that on a pub menu I'm out the door quicker than you can say 'pork belly and mustard mash'. I'm with Owain George, owner of The Albion in Bristol, when he says: 'If the chefs tried to put a foam on the menu here, I'd slap them round the head.'

The key elements in a good gastropub are energy and authenticity. A creative force hits you as soon as you open the door. They are run by people who are nuts about food. Some owners and chefs, such as the guys at The Wellington Arms in Hampshire, have the excitement of kids who are running their own sweet shop. Arrive there and they will tell you how good the trout – just delivered – is, and that the steamed apple pudding (accompanied by custard made with eggs from their own hens) is unmissable, and that the hens have been laying really well. Chef Steve Harris has a good phrase for it. I would sometimes phone him after I'd been to a new place and he would ask: 'So is it the real deal?' What he meant was, does it have a deep and unpretentious commitment to real food? Does it pulsate with the kind of energy and care which his mate Jim Shave brings to The Granville in Kent? Jim is capable of doing lunchtime service, going to the kitchen garden to put in a hundred leeks and then heading out for a spot of fishing. If he catches something it will be on the menu that night. You see, the Granville is the real deal. And those gastropubs that are rolled out in lots of six or seventy-five can never be.

My impression, after spending 18 months eating in them is that, far from getting worse, gastropubs are getting better. And that, at last, dining pubs are the place where British cookery is evolving and thriving. Of course Mediterranean stuff is on offer – it's popular and chefs are running businesses – but read some of the menus in our best dining pubs. Pea and ham soup, baked duck eggs with Somerset truffles, creamy Lancashire cheese and onion pie, braised oxtail with deep fried oysters, warm gooseberry and elderflower tart with Cornish clotted cream: it's great food.

To chef-owners and publicans I would say get rid of the fancy pants stuff. To diners and drinkers I say support good dining pubs, ignore the bad ones and don't damn gastropubs as a genre. Yes, there are bad examples. But there are cracking ones too. So prepare your tastebuds and enjoy one of the most positive developments in British dining in the last twenty years.

DIANA HENRY

the west country

Imagine Peter Cook with a penchant for good food and you're on your way to understanding the force behind The Albion. In most dining pubs it is chefs who are the driving force. Here the talents of owner Owain George and head chef Jake Platt are equally important.

Having been brought up in a supremely hospitable household ('there was always soup on the hob, just in case someone would turn up'), Owain seems compelled to provide a place which is a home from home. He even arranges for the streets nearby – a lovely enclave that includes a distinctive café and a great deli – to be closed to traffic so that the pub can host a 'village' fête (complete with eight bands) and a Christmas hog roast (with an organ providing the music for late night carol singing). 'I'd give complementary labradors if I could,' he smiles.

Running a design business that specializes in doing up restaurants, creating The Albion was Owain's liberating antidote to branding. He designed all the furniture – contemporary settles, chunky tables and leather armchairs – and had it made in his workshops. The result is homely but tasteful and the place breathes life. As soon as you enter from the courtyard outside you are confronted by a huge table of Albion produce – bread in all shapes and sizes, cured olives, jams and chutneys – and the smells of good food emanating from the small kitchen.

Jake spent his formative years under Stephen Marwick, a legend in the culinary history of the West Country, and Marwick's 'pure love of food', as Jake describes it, is clear in his approach. Jake's thing is simple food and what ends up on the plate – braised oxtail, roast turbot with Jerusalem artichokes and penny buns, wild salmon with braised lettuce and sorrel, Barkham blue rarebit with pickled walnuts – seems simple enough, but the oxtail, for example, takes 10 days to perfect and stocks are simmered to a Marmitey darkness.

Jake is happy that Owain gives him and his three sous-chefs free rein in the kitchen, though Owain keeps an eye on it all from a distance and doesn't like fancy stuff. 'If they tried to serve up food with foams,' he says bluntly, 'I'd smack them round the head.'

Owain and Jake are proud that most of their trade is walk-in, that there's enough of a foodie following for them to try out and sell unusual dishes (such as their 'three ways with a pig's head'), and that you can have lunch here for as little as six quid. Neither of them want The Albion to be a destination dining place, but it's worth the trip. You may even, after a visit, think it was worth moving to Bristol to make it your local.

the albion

BOYCES AVENUE, CLIFTON VILLAGE, BRISTOL, BS8 4AA • TEL 0117 973 3522 • www.thealbionclifton.co.uk
SERVES LUNCH (EXCEPT MONDAY) AND DINNER (EXCEPT MONDAY AND NO HOT FOOD SUNDAY EVENINGS)

serves 8–10

2 HEADS OF FENNEL

200ML (7FL OZ) OLIVE OIL

350G (12OZ) SMOKED HADDOCK
  FILLET, SKIN REMOVED

2 LARGE ONIONS, FINELY CHOPPED

4 CELERY STICKS, DICED

½ CUCUMBER, DESEEDED AND DICED

1 LEEK, CLEANED AND SLICED

GENEROUS PINCH OF SAFFRON

1 TSP CUMIN SEEDS

1 TSP CORIANDER SEEDS

1 TSP FENNEL SEEDS

1 SMALL DRIED RED CHILLI

2 400G CANS CHOPPED TOMATOES

4 BAY LEAVES

½ BOTTLE (375ML/13FL OZ) DRY
  WHITE WINE

2 LITRES (3½PTS) FISH STOCK

BUNCH OF BASIL

BUNCH OF CORIANDER

SMALL BUNCH OF DILL

BUNCH OF FLAT-LEAF PARSLEY

SMALL BUNCH OF TARRAGON

LEMON JUICE, TO TASTE

4 GENEROUS TBSP AÏOLI

1.5KG (3LB) CHUNKY WHITE FISH
  (SUCH AS POLLOCK, HADDOCK,
  COD OR GURNARD, OR A MIXTURE),
  SKINNED, FILLETED AND CUT INTO
  LARGE CHUNKS

500G (1LB 2OZ) MUSSELS, CLEANED

SALT AND PEPPER

TO FINISH

OLIVE OIL, FOR FRYING

8–10 SMALL FILLETS RED MULLET
  OR BREAM

SALT AND PEPPER

BREAD, ROUILLE AND AÏOLI, TO SERVE

the albion's fish stew

This is a fantastic dish for a big lunch or supper party. Serve with aïoli and rouille, the classic Provençal accompaniments.

Prepare the base of the stew (this can be done in advance). Quarter the fennel lengthways, discard the central core and dice the remaining flesh. In a large, heavy-based pan, heat the oil until it is almost smoking and fry the smoked haddock until it is crisp. Reduce the heat, add all of the prepared vegetables and cook until soft but not coloured (10–15 minutes). Add the spices and cook for a further 2 minutes then add the tomatoes and bay leaves and simmer until the tomato juice has really reduced. Add the wine, bring to the boil and reduce by half. Pour on the fish stock, bring up to the boil and then reduce by half. Finish with the herbs (use just the leaves, roughly chopped) and season with lemon juice.

Heat the soup base to boiling point then whisk in the aïoli off the heat. Don't bring the mixture to the boil after adding the aïoli or it will curdle. Tap the mussel shells with a knife, discarding any that do not close. Add the white fish and the mussels and poach in the soup, covered, until the mussels open. Discard any that do not open. Taste for seasoning – the wine, smoked haddock and mussels all make the stew salty so you probably won't need to add any salt. Heat some olive oil in a frying pan and cook the mullet or bream fillets, skin-side down, for 1 minute. Season, turn the heat down low and cook for another minute. Turn over and cook for a futher minute. Spoon the stew into bowls and top each with a fillet. Serve with bread and rouille and some aïoli.

aïoli

3 EGG YOLKS
JUICE OF 1 LEMON
2TSP DIJON MUSTARD
3 CLOVES GARLIC, CRUSHED
SALT AND PEPPER
200ML (7FL OZ) OLIVE OIL

Put the egg yolks, lemon juice, mustard, garlic and salt and pepper into a blender or food processor and blitz (you can use a hand-beater if your processor is too big).

With the motor running, slowly add the oil, little by little, allowing the mixture to thicken before adding the next drop. Keep adding the oil until everything has come together and the aïoli has emulsified. Taste for seasoning.

rouille

1 THICK SLICE COUNTRY BREAD
FISH STOCK (OR WATER)
2 CLOVES GARLIC
1 ROASTED RED PEPPER
2 SMALL FRESH RED CHILLIES
2 EGG YOLKS
1TSP DIJON MUSTARD
250ML (8FL OZ) OLIVE OIL

Remove the crusts from the bread, soak in fish stock (or water), then squeeze dry. Finely chop the garlic. Skin and deseed the red pepper. Deseed and finely chop the chillies.

Put all of these into a food processor, along with the egg yolks and mustard. Slowly add the oil until it has all been incorporated and the mixture is thick. Taste for seasoning.

'Owain has even arranged for the streets nearby – a lovely enclave including a distinctive café and a great deli – to be closed to traffic so the pub can host a "village" fête (complete with eight bands) and a Christmas hog roast (with an organ providing the music for late night carol singing). "I'd give complementary labradors if I could", he smiles.'

serves 4

100G (3½OZ) UNSALTED BUTTER

100G (3½OZ) FRESH MOREL MUSHROOMS,
 CAREFULLY CLEANED OF SOIL AND DIRT

1 CLOVE GARLIC, VERY FINELY CHOPPED

2TSP FINELY CHOPPED FLAT-LEAF PARSLEY

4 DUCK EGGS

SALT AND PEPPER

4 SLICES BRIOCHE

1 BLACK OR WHITE TRUFFLE
 (ABOUT 10G/⅓OZ IN WEIGHT)

baked duck egg with wild mushrooms
& somerset truffle

Jake manages to get his hands on Somerset truffles for this dish but any truffle
will do, should you be lucky enough to procure one.

Preheat the oven to 170°C/325°F/gas mark 3. Melt 75g (3oz) of the butter in a frying pan and,
when foaming, add the mushrooms and garlic and fry for 2 minutes. Throw in the parsley and mix.

Spoon the mixture into 4 ramekins or small gratin dishes and break the eggs on top. Season and
top each egg with a knob of the remaining butter. Put into the oven and bake for 6 minutes or
until just set. Toast the brioche.

Shave the truffle over the top of the baked eggs and serve with the toasted brioche.

serves 4

OIL, FOR FRYING

3 LARGE WHITE ONIONS,
    FINELY SLICED

6–8 SPRIGS OF THYME

2 CLOVES GARLIC, CRUSHED

8 WHITE PEPPERCORNS

4 BAY LEAVES

500ML (18FL OZ) DRY CIDER,
    SUCH AS WESTON'S OR ANY WEST
    COUNTRY CIDER

500ML (18FL OZ) GOOD STRONG
    CHICKEN STOCK

4 HANDFULS OF HAY (OBTAINABLE
    FROM ANY PET SHOP)

250G (9OZ) PORK BELLY

2 STAR ANISE

12 STONED AGEN PRUNES, SOAKED
    OVERNIGHT IN PORT OR TEA

A 4-BONE RACK OF PORK, FRENCH
    TRIMMED AND ROLLED

SALT AND WHITE PEPPER

8 THICK SLICES OF BLACK PUDDING

sharing dish of louise cook's pork

Some pubs now serve dishes-to-share when dishes can only be sensibly cooked
for more than one person. This is one such case. At The Albion you order this
and wait in shared greedy anticipation...and the addition of hay is correct. It's
an old method and does impart a certain flavour.

Prepare the pork belly first. Preheat the oven to 130°C/250°F/gas mark ½. Heat 3tbsp oil in a
large heavy-based saucepan and cook the onions slowly with the thyme, garlic, peppercorns and
bay leaves until nicely soft and brown; this could take as long as 30 minutes. Keep the heat low
and add a splash of water every so often. Add the cider and boil to reduce by half, then add the
chicken stock. Put half the hay into a casserole and put the pork belly and star anise on top. Pour
over the onion and stock mixture, cover with the rest of the hay and a tight-fitting lid. Cook in the
oven for 1 hour, or until a knife can be inserted with no resistance. Take the pork out, brush off
the hay, leave to cool then remove the bones and skin. Tear the meat into large pieces. Pour the
liquid out of the casserole then strain to remove the onions and any bits of hay. Put into a clean
pan and reduce by half or until it has a sauce-like consistency. Add the prunes to the torn bits of
pork and moisten with some cooking juices, leaving the rest of the sauce to serve once you've
cooked the rack of pork. This part of the recipe can be done up to two days in advance.

Finally, cook the rack of pork. Preheat the oven to 200°C/400°F/gas mark 6. Rub the skin with
salt and white pepper. Heat 3tbsp of oil in a large pan and brown evenly all over. Place in a
roasting tin, skin-side up, and roast for 30 minutes. Rest the pork (covered with foil and insulated
with tea towels) for 15 minutes. Heat 2tbsp oil in a frying pan and fry the black pudding over
a medium heat until cooked through – about 5 minutes on each side. Heat the pork belly with
prunes and the sauce. Serve the rack of pork, belly with prunes, sauce and black pudding. It's
good with apple sauce and greens on the side.

serves 2–3

FOR THE OXTAIL

1KG (2LB) OXTAIL, JOINTED

SMALL BUNCH OF THYME

6 BAY LEAVES

6 SHALLOTS, SLICED

4 CLOVES GARLIC, CRUSHED

1 BOTTLE GOOD RED WINE

2TBSP DUCK FAT OR BEEF DRIPPING

SALT AND PEPPER

200G (7OZ) BACON LARDONS

STOCK OR WATER

6 NEW POTATOES, PARBOILED
AND SCRAPED

8 JERUSALEM ARTICHOKES, PEELED
AND LEFT WHOLE

4 PARSNIPS, CORED AND
CUT INTO LARGE PIECES

2TBSP DUCK FAT

6 SPRIGS OF THYME

SALT AND PEPPER

1 RIB STEAK WITH THE
BONE ATTACHED, APPROXIMATELY
400G (14OZ)

2TBSP VEGETABLE OIL

SALT AND PEPPER

roast rib of beef with braised oxtail & roast veg

This is a feast. You need to prepare the oxtail in advance so that you only have the beef and vegetables to cook on the day you want to serve it. At The Albion, they also serve the dish accompanied by beetroot that has been baked in coarse salt with garlic and rosemary.

Put the oxtail pieces into a tight-fitting container with the herbs, shallots, garlic and enough wine to cover. Leave in the fridge for 3–5 days. Preheat the oven to 150°C/300°F/gas mark 2. Take the oxtail out of the marinade, reserving the herbs, shallots and garlic.

Heat the fat in a large casserole and brown the oxtail pieces until brown all over. Remove and season with salt and pepper. In the same pan cook the shallots, garlic and bacon until golden. Add the rest of the red wine, bring to the boil and reduce by a third. Now add the oxtail pieces and enough stock to cover them. Bring to the boil, skim the surface and after reducing the heat, put into the oven. Cook for 2 hours, or until the meat is really tender and almost falling off the bone. Leave the oxtail to cool and then place in the fridge until you want to serve it with the rest of the dish.

Preheat the oven to 200°C/400°F/gas mark 6. Put the vegetables and the fat into a roasting tin and add the thyme and seasoning. Roast until nicely browned (about 20–30 minutes), turning regularly.

Heat the oil in a frying pan and brown the rib of beef all over. Season and roast in the oven for 15 minutes. Cover in foil and insulate with tea towels, and leave to rest for 10–15 minutes. Heat the oxtail. Carve the beef and serve with the braised oxtail and roasted vegetables.

serves 4

FOR THE ICE-CREAM
200G (7FL OZ) GRANULATED SUGAR
100ML (3½ FL OZ) WATER
400ML (14FL OZ) MILK
400ML (14FL OZ) DOUBLE CREAM
200G (7OZ) SALTED BUTTER
10G (⅓ OZ) CORNFLOUR
6 EGG YOLKS
20ML (¾ FL OZ) LIQUID GLUCOSE

8 JUST RIPE, SWEET BLACK FIGS,
   CUT IN HALF
50G (1¾ OZ) UNSALTED BUTTER
4 SLICES BRIOCHE, HALVED
2 EGGS
150G (5½ OZ) CASTER SUGAR
A DROP OF VANILLA EXTRACT
4 GENEROUS TSP HONEY IN
   THE COMB

roast black figs, brown butter ice-cream, honeycomb & brioche

This is a very unusual ice-cream – I've never come across anything like it before – and feel very lucky that Jake was willing to part with the recipe.

To make the ice-cream, put the sugar and water into a pan and heat slowly, stirring gently from time to time. When the sugar has dissolved, whack up the heat, bring to the boil and keep it boiling until it caramelizes – be careful not to let it burn. Take off the heat and put the base of the pan into cold water. Mix the milk and cream in another pan. Add the caramel and gently bring up to the boil, stirring to make sure the mixture is smooth, then take off the heat.

Heat the butter in a saucepan until it is a nutty brown colour – be careful, again, not to go too far. The smell should be toasty and the colour not too dark. Strain through a sieve into a small bowl and whisk in the cornflour until you have a smooth mixture. Whisk the yolks and glucose together until pale in colour and much increased in volume. Whisk in the butter and cornflour mixture, then half of the milk and cream mixture. Put into a heavy-based pan with the remaining milk and cream mixture and cook over a low heat, stirring, until it has slightly thickened (it should coat the back of a spoon). Do not allow the mixture to boil. Strain through a sieve then cool and chill. Churn in an ice-cream machine or freeze in a shallow container, beating the mixture every couple of hours to break up the crystals that are forming and to incorporate air.

To put the dessert together, heat a pan big enough to hold all the figs in a single layer. Melt 15g (½ oz) butter and heat until it foams, then add the figs and turn in the hot butter until they're warmed through. Set aside. Beat the eggs, sugar and vanilla together and put the brioche slices into it. Let them soak for about 2 minutes then turn the pieces over and soak the other side too. In another pan, heat the remaining butter until it foams and fry the brioche slices for about 1 minute on each side, until the pieces are golden and you can see that the eggy mixture has cooked. Serve the warm figs on top of the brioche with a good scoop of ice-cream and some fresh honeycomb.

serves 8

FOR THE ICE-CREAM
600ML (1 PINT) STOUT
150ML (¼ PINT) FULL FAT MILK
450ML (¾ PINT) DOUBLE CREAM
1 VANILLA POD, SPLIT ALONG
    ITS LENGTH
6 EGG YOLKS
125G (4OZ) CASTER SUGAR

FOR THE CHOCOLATE FONDANT
225G (8OZ) PLAIN CHOCOLATE, WITH 70%
    COCOA SOLIDS, BROKEN INTO PIECES
225G (8OZ) UNSALTED BUTTER, PLUS A
    LITTLE EXTRA FOR GREASING THE
    DARIOLE MOULDS
3 EGGS
3 EGG YOLKS
90G (3½OZ) CASTER SUGAR
25G (1OZ) PLAIN FLOUR

bitter chocolate fondant with stout ice-cream

Stout and chocolate are a marriage made in heaven.

To make the ice-cream, bring the stout up to the boil and let it bubble away until you have just 100ml (3½ fl oz) of liquid left. Put the milk, cream and vanilla pod in a pan and bring to the boil then take off the heat and leave so that the vanilla can infuse and flavour the cream mixture.

Beat the egg yolks and sugar together until very pale and thick. Remove the vanilla pod from the infused cream (wash, dry and use again for something else) and pour the cream on to the beaten eggs. Put into a heavy-based saucepan and cook over a gentle heat, stirring continuously, until the mixture has thickened (it should coat the back of a spoon). Do not let the mixture boil or it will curdle. Pour through a sieve and leave to cool, then add the reduced stout. Chill the mixture, then churn in an ice-cream machine following the manufacturer's instructions, or freeze in a shallow container in the freezer, whisking the mixture every couple of hours as it freezes to break up the crystals and incorporate air.

Lightly butter 8 x 6cm (3 x 2½ inch) dariole moulds for the chocolate fondants. Set a bowl over a pan of simmering water (the bottom of the bowl should be in steam, not in water) and put the chocolate and butter into the bowl. Melt, stirring from time to time to help it along. Leave sitting – you want it to stay warm. Whisk the whole eggs and egg yolks together with the sugar until the mixture has quadrupled in size. Add the flour. Carefully fold in the chocolate mixture, trying to avoid knocking out too much air. Divide between the dariole moulds and chill for 40 minutes. Preheat the oven to 190°C/375°F/gas mark 5.

Bake the chocolate fondants for 8 minutes. Leave in the moulds to rest for 1 minute. Run a very fine knife between the edges of the mould and the edge of the pudding, then invert the moulds onto plates and turn the puddings out. Serve with a scoop of the ice-cream.

It is a Saturday morning in early September. At The Gurnard's Head, a few walkers nurse pints in the bar while others cradle mugs of tea. The remnants of breakfast – the day's papers, pots of coffee and jars of homemade jam – lie lazily on the huge table in the dining room. There's a patch of bright blue sea beyond the fields and the local hunt (no longer hunting but still going for weekend rides) has pitched up outside. The riders are chatting to the postman and taking delivery of tray upon tray of drinks.

All in all, it's a genuine image of British rural life. How do Charles and Edmund Inkin do it? Together they own and run two dining pubs, The Felin Fach Griffin in Wales and now this Cornish gem. And in both they have created oases of civility and warmth, places where both urbanites and locals feel at home.

The Gurnard is large – it looks like a big old manor house, not a cosy little pub – and was a bit of a wreck when the Inkins bought it. They've spruced it up in their inimitable style; they know what to change and what to leave alone. The dining rooms sport a terra cotta and Yves Klein-blue colour scheme, but the bar itself – one of those varnished tongue and groove affairs that seemed bad-taste in the '70s and now have a kind of retro-chic – has barely been touched and the shelves behind it are a glorious muddle of postcards, mugs and knick-knacks. It's a place that is comfortable with itself and the credit for this must go to Charles. He is that rare and valued phenomenon: a proprietor who is a true original. He's a charmer, a bit of a rogue (ladies beware) and very English to boot (think Jack Nicholson, but educated at Eton).

The general approach leads you to expect the food to be great, and you aren't disappointed. It's simple, clean, modern (without being modish) country cooking, bursting with flavour. The chefs – Kiwi Matthew Williamson set the style and Rob Wright has picked up the baton – don't muck about: dishes such as fish stew with fennel flowers, oat-rolled pork belly with rhubarb, split pea and pumpkin soup, skate with pancetta, parsley and sherry vinaigrette and elderflower fritters with gooseberry sorbet show off great ingredients. In general it owes much to the spirit of Californian cookery. Samphire, wild garlic and mushrooms are foraged by Caroline Arkley. The salad leaves and veg are collected from a grower within walking distance every morning, and the meat and fish are local.

The Gurnard's Head feels as if it's being looked after by teenagers (responsible ones) while the parents are away – it's youthful, chilled out, life-affirming. You'll leave with a smile on your face.

the gurnard's head

TREEN, CORNWALL, TR26 3DE • TEL 01736 796928 • www.gurnardshead.co.uk
SERVES LUNCH AND DINNER EVERY DAY, ROOMS AVAILABLE

serves 4

8 FRESH SARDINES, GUTTED AND SCALED
1 TBSP OLIVE OIL

FOR THE RELISH
HANDFUL OF RAISINS (ABOUT 25G/1OZ)
2 MEDIUM BEETROOT, UNCOOKED
1 TBSP MUSTARD SEEDS
1 TBSP FRESHLY GRATED HORSERADISH
1 TBSP GOOD QUALITY RED WINE VINEGAR
SALT AND PEPPER

grilled sardines with beetroot relish

Mackerel take very well to this treatment too.

Begin by making your relish. Pour a cup of boiling water over the raisins and leave to soak for 30 minutes. Cut the beetroot into thin matchsticks, ideally using a mandolin (or else use a food processor, grater or sharp knife). Add the mustard seeds, horseradish, red wine vinegar and plumped-up raisins. Taste the mix and season judiciously, remembering you want a fairly peppy, confident relish to go alongside your sardines.

Turn your grill on to full heat and place a flat roasting tray underneath until it is scorching hot.

Season the sardines inside and out and oil both sides of the flesh. Place the sardines side by side on the hot tray. If they sizzle, they won't stick! Depending on size, grill the sardines for about 3 minutes on each side. The flesh should be just opaque and the meat should just pull away from the spine. Serve the sardines with a little pile of the relish.

'The Gurnard's Head feels as if it's being looked after by teenagers (responsible ones) while the parents are away – it is youthful, chilled out, life-affirming. You'll leave with a smile on your face.'

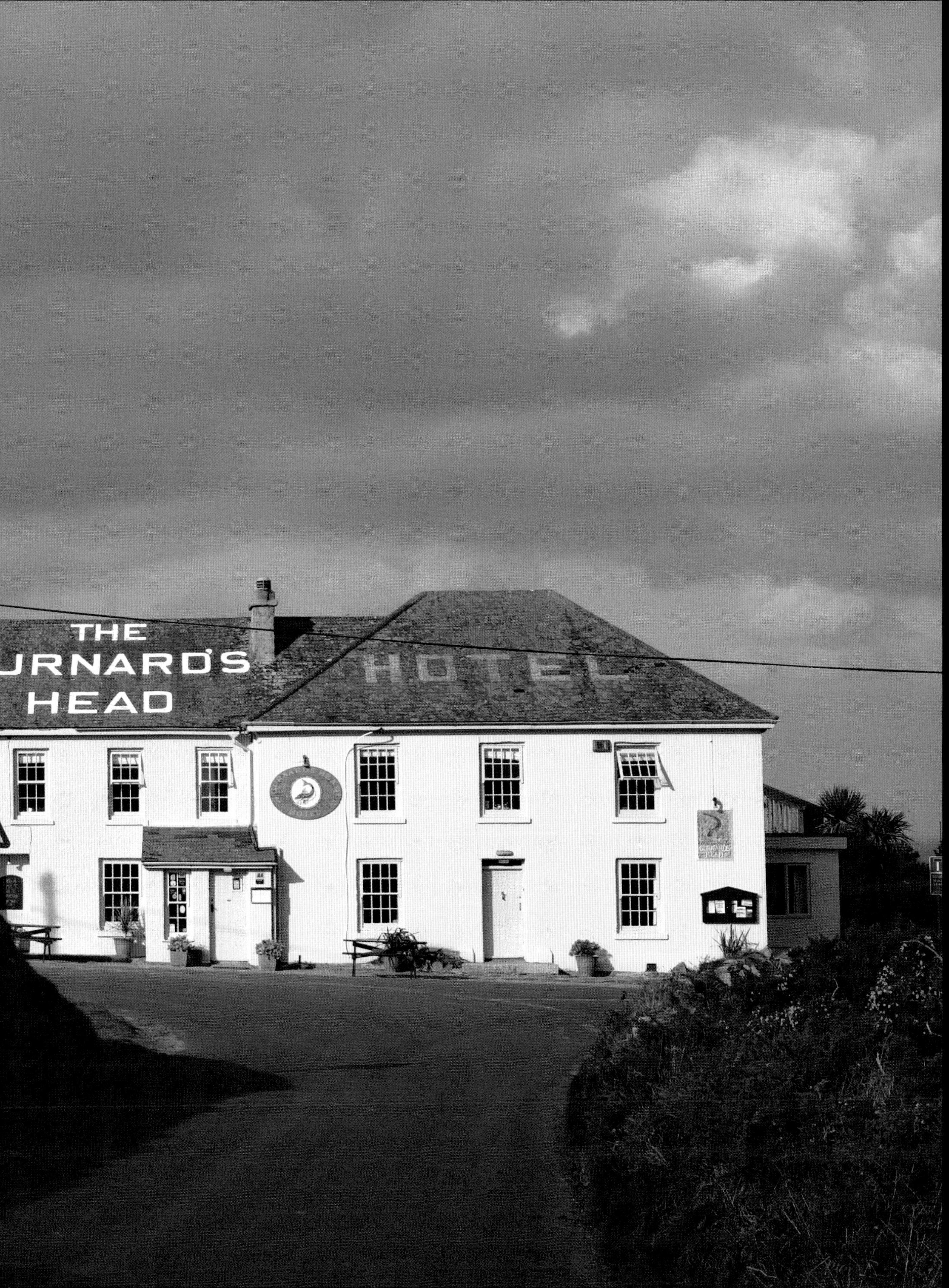
THE
URNARD'S
HEAD
HOTEL

serves 4

FOR THE CURED DUCK BREAST
2 CARDAMOM PODS
8 CORIANDER SEEDS
1 STRIP ORANGE RIND
½ VANILLA POD
1 BAY LEAF
4 BLACK PEPPERCORNS

1 TBSP SEA SALT
1 LARGE DUCK BREAST, TRIMMED
  OF ALL ITS SINEWS

FOR THE DAMSON CHEESE
DAMSONS
WATER
GRANULATED SUGAR

cured duck breast with damson cheese

You need at least 10 days' forward planning for this dish.

In a pestle and mortar (or a spice grinder), pound together the cardamom, coriander, orange rind, vanilla, bay leaf, peppercorns and salt. Rub this mixture vigorously into the duck breast, ensuring every bit of flesh and fat has been well covered. Brush off any excess spice mixture and neatly wrap and tie the duck breast in some muslin (or a piece of cheesecloth or a totally clean tea towel). Secure one end with some string and hang the breast, not in contact with anything else, in the fridge (or cellar or a cold outhouse) for at least 10 days. The breast is ready to use when the meat feels like a steak that is between medium to well-cooked. To test, press your wedding ring finger against the pad of flesh beneath your thumb – the duck breast should have the same resistance. This will keep, wrapped, in the fridge for a couple of weeks.

To make the damson cheese, rinse, de-stalk and weigh your damsons. For every 1kg (2lb 4oz) of damsons, measure out 150ml (¼ pint) of water. In a large preserving pan, simmer the fruit with the water until pulpy and soft. Mash the fruit, push it through a sieve and measure out the pulp. You will need 350g (12oz) of sugar for every 500ml (18fl oz) of purée. Put the sugar and fruit pulp back into the cleaned preserving pan and simmer over a very low heat until the sugar has dissolved, stirring occasionally. Turn the heat up to more of a moderate bubble and evaporate most of the liquid. The damson cheese is ready when a wooden spoon drawn through the mixture leaves a split-second parting in the bottom of the pan. This may take some time and the pan will be prone to spluttering hot damson bubbles so be careful. Pour the mixture into a terrine dish (or any square or oblong heat-resistant container), cool and leave to set in the fridge. The cheese can be sliced as and when needed. It will keep, covered in the fridge, for many months.

At The Gurnard they serve this with celeriac remoulade, made by cutting a small head of celeriac into matchsticks, salted for 30 minutes to draw out the moisture, squeezed and then dressed with 4tbsp crème fraîche, 1tbsp Dijon mustard, a squeeze of lemon and salt and pepper.

Cut the duck breast into thin slices and divide between 4 plates. Put a slice of damson cheese and a pile of remoulade with each serving.

serves 6

FOR THE BASIC RISOTTO	TO MAKE IT INTERESTING
1 TBSP OLIVE OIL	2 WHOLE HEADS GARLIC
3 SHALLOTS, FINELY CHOPPED	SALT AND PEPPER
½ HEAD OF CELERY, FINELY CHOPPED	OLIVE OIL
2 CLOVES GARLIC, FINELY CHOPPED	3 TBSP FLAKED OR WHOLE ALMONDS
400G (14OZ) RISOTTO RICE	A VERY GENEROUS KNOB OF BUTTER
2 X 125ML GLASSES DRY WHITE WINE	5 TBSP FRESHLY GRATED PARMESAN CHEESE
1.2 LITRES (2 PINTS) CHICKEN STOCK	2 TBSP FRESH THYME LEAVES
SALT AND PEPPER	JUICE OF ABOUT ½ LEMON (TO TASTE)

almond, thyme & roasted garlic risotto

For perfect consistency, the risotto should almost move to the other side of the plate as you place the dish in front of your guest.

Start with the interesting addition: the roasted garlic and toasted almonds. Preheat the oven to 180°C/350°F/gas mark 4. Halve the garlic across its belly and season generously with salt and pepper and drizzle with olive oil. Place the garlic halves in a tightly sealed but loosely fitting parcel of foil. Roast for 40 minutes or until the garlic cloves are soft enough to squash between finger and thumb. Toast the almonds in a small pan over a medium-low heat until sandy-coloured (about 3 minutes), watching all the time that they do not burn, then set aside.

Now begin the risotto. Heat the olive oil in a large pan and over a moderate heat gently sweat the shallots, celery and garlic until soft but not coloured. Add the risotto rice. Mix and cook for 2 minutes or so, until the rice turns translucent. Add the white wine (you should hear your pan exhale when you do this) and mix thoroughly until the liquid has all but evaporated.

Reduce the heat and start adding the stock to the rice, ladleful by ladleful, stirring all the time. Ensure that each measure of liquid has been absorbed before you add the next. Towards the end, check the texture of the rice – you want it to be al dente. It should be ready in 16–18 minutes.

Gently squeeze the garlic halves so the flesh oozes out of the skins. Add the roasted garlic flesh to the risotto pan and then add the knob of butter, 3 tablespoons of the Parmesan and the thyme leaves. Give the pan a thorough stir and put a lid on the pan. Leave to rest for at least 5 minutes.

To finish your risotto, check for seasoning, adding salt, pepper and lemon juice as needed. Serve in wide bowls or plates and scatter each dish with toasted almonds and Parmesan.

serves 4

HANDFUL OF COARSE SEA SALT

2 MEDIUM-SIZED BEETROOT, UNCOOKED

1KG (2LB 4OZ) FILLET OF BEEF, CUT INTO 4 FAT STEAKS

SALT

1TSP SUNFLOWER OIL

FOR THE BEIGNETS

75G (2½OZ) STRONG WHITE FLOUR

PINCH OF SALT

115ML (3½FL OZ) WATER

55G (2OZ) BUTTER, CUT INTO 1CM/½ INCH CUBES

2–3 EGGS

1TBSP FRESHLY GRATED HORSERADISH

1TSP MUSTARD POWDER

SUNFLOWER OIL, FOR DEEP-FRYING

FOR THE WATERCRESS MAYONNAISE

250G (9OZ) WATERCRESS, PLUS EXTRA FOR SERVING

1 EGG YOLK

½TSP DIJON MUSTARD

110ML (3½FL OZ) OIL: A MIX OF 30 ML (1FL OZ) OLIVE OIL
AND 80ML (2½FL OZ) SUNFLOWER OIL

1½ TSP WHITE WINE VINEGAR

SALT AND PEPPER

beef fillet with beetroot, horseradish beignets & watercress mayonnaise

I love to find recipes that present a familiar ingredient – here fillet of beef –
a bit differently without doing anything really complicated. This is a great dish
for spring, summer and autumn.

Preheat the oven to 180°C/350°F/gas mark 4. Scatter a handful of sea salt into a roasting
tin and lay the beetroot among it. Cover the entire tin with foil and put in the oven for
40 minutes, or until you can pierce the beetroot fairly effortlessly with a skewer. (You can roast
the beetroot in advance and reheat it when needed. But, as with most things, it's far nicer
freshly cooked.

To make the watercress mayonnaise, pick the leaves from the bunch of watercress and pour boiling water over the leaves. Count to three then drain and plunge the leaves into ice-cold water. Drain once again, squeezing the leaves quite tightly to remove any excess water, and blitz the green mass in a food processor until smooth.

Put the yolk in a high-sided bowl and add the Dijon mustard. Then ever so gently – dribble by dribble – start adding the oils, whisking all the time. When the mixture begins to thicken, add some of the vinegar to loosen the consistency. Continue with the oil and finish with the remaining vinegar. Taste the mayonnaise and season with salt and pepper. Finally, stir through the watercress purée and taste once more. If you feel the mayonnaise is too thick, add dribbles of cold water to loosen it.

For the beignets, the choux pastry can be made in advance, refrigerated, and then balled up and deep-fried when you are in the final throes of cooking your steaks. Sieve the flour and salt on to a sheet of greaseproof paper. Heat the water with the butter until the butter has melted. Boil quickly and remove from the heat. Tip the flour into the saucepan and beat thoroughly until the mixture is smooth and begins to come away from the sides of the pan and form a ball. Place the pan back on a moderate heat, mixing continuously and watching for when the mixture begins to fur the bottom of the saucepan. Remove from the heat and cool for 2 minutes.

Crack the eggs and separate the yolks into a separate bowl. Add one yolk at a time to the dough mixture, beating vigorously each time to ensure the yolk is integrated and the mixture looks as it did before you added the first yolk. The pastry is ready when the dough begins to lose its capacity to form a cohesive ball in the centre of the pan and drops reluctantly from a spoon. Mix in the grated horseradish and mustard powder. Set the mixture aside; you cook the beignets at the last minute, while the steaks are resting.

To cook the steaks, rub the flesh with the oil and season with salt (pepper will burn in the searing of the meat, so it's best left until the meat is resting). Heat a frying pan until it's very hot. Place the steaks in the pan to sear the meat. Fry each steak on both sides until done to your liking. In an ideal world, the steak should rest for longer than you've cooked it. To rest it, cover it with foil and insulate with a couple of tea towels.

If you have cooked your beetroot in advance reheat it now – either in the oven or quickly sauté in a little butter in a frying pan. To cook the beignets, heat the neutral-tasting sunflower oil in a pan until very hot (190°C/375°F). Using 2 dessertspoons, drop walnut-sized balls of dough (these will be fairly randomly shaped) into the oil. They are ready when they rise to the top and float for a few seconds. Drain on kitchen paper and season with a sprinkle of salt.

Serve the steaks with the beignets, the beetroot and the watercress mayonnaise, with an extra pile of fresh watercress alongside.

serves 8
3 LEAVES GELATINE
400ML (14FL OZ) DOUBLE CREAM
250G (9OZ) CASTER SUGAR
4 THINLY PARED STRIPS OF LEMON RIND
600ML (1 PINT) BUTTERMILK
2TSP ROSEWATER
RASPBERRIES AND ROSE PETALS, TO SERVE

rose buttermilk pudding with raspberries

When roses are at their headiest and their scent sends you reeling, you can use fresh petals instead of rosewater – just leave the petals to infuse in the cream. Likewise, you could place a few petals in the bottom of each mould for decoration when turned out. If you are nervous about unmoulding then set the puddings in pretty glasses.

Place the gelatine in a shallow bowl and cover with cold water.

Gently heat half the double cream along with the sugar and lemon rind in a saucepan over a low heat. When just about to boil, remove; cover the pan with a lid and leave to infuse for 10 minutes.

Whisk the gelatine into the infused cream and strain the mixture through a sieve into a clean bowl. Add the buttermilk and rosewater.

Gently whip the remaining double cream and fold this through the buttermilk mixture. Pour into 8 dariole moulds and leave them to set in the fridge (it takes about 4 hours). Unmould the puddings onto plates when set. Serve with raspberries and rose petals, with shortbread biscuits on the side.

serves 8
4 PEACHES
75G (3OZ) UNSALTED BUTTER
ABOUT 16 BRANCHES FRESH THYME, PLUS
  4 FOR INFUSED HONEY
8TBSP HONEY, PLUS 2–3TBSP FOR DRIZZLING
8 SLICES GORGONZOLA CHEESE, QUANTITY
  ACCORDING TO TASTE

gorgonzola cheese with thyme-infused honey & roast peaches

A very simple and achingly pretty dish. It's important that its components are served at room temperature.

Preheat the oven to 200°C/400°F/gas mark 6. Halve and stone the peaches and sit them comfortably together, cut-side up, in an ovenproof dish. Place a generous knob of butter and some whole branches of thyme on each peach half. Drizzle with honey and roast until the flesh seems just about to collapse and the peaches are nicely caramelized – how long this takes depends on their ripeness, but reckon on 15 minutes or so.

Going on 1tbsp of honey per person and ½ branch of thyme each, put more honey in a saucepan with the thyme. Gently heat, but don't boil, for 10 minutes. Leave to cool.

Place a piece of gorgonzola on each plate, drizzle with the cooled infused honey and place half a peach on each plate.

the best of the rest

the chasers

When I wrote my first book on dining pubs, chef Darren Bunn was cooking at The Greyhound in Stockbridge and a wonderful job he was doing, too. I was sorry when he left, but now he has opened his own pub, in all its thatched glory, hidden among a network of leafy Devon lanes. And his cooking is as good as ever. His background is classical, and it shows, but he brings a light, modern touch and dishes are just the right side of complicated: terrine of ham hock, foie gras and potato with celeriac remoulade or Brixham sea bass with butter beans and chorizo are fab and puds are more unusual than you often find in dining pubs. Chocolate terrine with orange marmalade ice-cream is divine. Sensibly, he offers a great ploughman's lunch with West Country cheddar, something too many dining pubs think themselves too grand to provide.

Stoke Road, Stokeinteignhead, Devon, TQ12 4QS Tel. 01626 873670, www.thechasers.co.uk Serves lunch (except Monday) and dinner (except Sunday and Monday).

the jack in the green inn

You don't quite expect what you get here. It seems like a pleasant enough place on the outside – the kind of gaff where you think you'd find decent scampi and chips – but nothing about the interior, which is pretty corporate, gets your hopes up. But the fact that the place is heaving should give the game away. And then the food arrives. It is perfectly judged, full of flavour, refined. Risottos are knock-out, noodle dishes terrific and the more complicated restauranty dishes – rack of lamb with artichokes, spring greens and almond tarragon dressing or sea bass with crab and braised baby gems – are spot on. Care is taken with every dish, particularly with seasoning and the use of decent ingredients. An exemplary food pub.

Rockbeare, Exeter, Devon, EX5 2EE Tel. 01404 822240, www.jackinthegreen.uk.com Serves lunch and dinner every day.

the kings arms

This is a splendid looking place, an 18th-century pub with a gorgeous ornate, cast-iron balcony. It's a fitting environment for the chef Rob Dawson's assured cooking. His ways with fish have made The King's Arms a destination dining pub, though there are still plenty who come just to down a pint in the bar. You'll find both modern dishes from all over the world and classical dishes – Thai fishcakes with mango and coconut salad, scallops and lentils with a rich Pedro Ximénez sherry syrup, Provençal fish soup or grilled Start Bay lobster with Café de Paris butter. There's Devon beef and Creedy Carver duck for the less piscine inclined. Puds are excellent too, witness Pimms jelly with a cucumber and mint sorbet. Great to see a British chef making so much of the fish right on his doorstep. Definitely worth the detour.

Dartmouth Road, Strete, Dartmouth, Devon, TQ6 0RW Tel. 01803 770377, www.kingsarms-dartmouth.co.uk Serves lunch every day and dinner (except Sunday and closed all day Monday in the winter).

the nobody inn

This has always been a crazy kind of place, in the best way – eccentric, jumbled, cheese-oriented – a definite one-off. The previous owner, Nick Borst-Smith, sold it on in early 2008 and experienced publicans Andy and Rowena Whiteman have taken it over. Though they are refurbishing the bedrooms and putting in a new kitchen, they are committed to preserving the character of the place, and especially want to maintain its reputation as a pub specializing in wine, whiskies and cheeses (there are bottles on every available space in the bar, a big selection of wines and no fewer than 260 different whiskies on offer). The food is good and as much as possible is sourced locally – fish, eel from Dartmouth, Devon beef and, of course, the cheeses, of which there are normally around 15 available. To enjoy a wonderfully original place it's worth the detour. Pretty as a picture village, too.

Doddiscombsleigh, Exeter, Devon, EX6 7PS Tel. 01647 252394, www.nobodyinn.co.uk Serves lunch every day and dinner (except Sunday), rooms available.

the normandy arms

People come from far and wide to eat the food served up here by chef Peter Alcroft. He cooked at the Dorchester in his earlier days and was previously chef-patron of the highly respected Blue Ball at Triscombe. Now in this white-washed pub (called the Normandy Arms because of the landings) he treats his fans to local fish, meat and game – beef carpaccio, pigeon with lentils, sea bass with gnocchi and broad beans – and the best West Country cheeses. All this in a lovely space with a slate bar – where drinkers are absolutely as important as diners – deep-red seating and low beams. Both Peter and co-owner Sharon Murdoch put their heart and soul into the Normandy. There's a lovely warm glow about the place.

Chapel Street, Blackawton, Totnes, Devon, TQ9 7BN Tel. 01803 712884. Serves lunch (except Monday) and dinner (except Sunday and Monday).

the farmer's inn

A rambling 16th-century inn surrounded by fields, this is one of the best places in the book for a pubby weekend away. The bar is still properly pub-like, with West Country ciders as well as ales available, and has gorgeous exposed stone walls and spindle-backed chairs. The dining room, though separate (there are two menus, one for the bar and one for the dining room) is still totally informal country in style with farmhouse furniture and no nappery. Food is modern British and resolutely seasonal. Beautifully presented too. Enjoy hot smoked salmon fillet with horseradish cream and crushed pink fir potatoes, loin of venison with chestnuts and Madeira or fig-stuffed guineafowl with savoy cabbage and bacon. And the bedrooms – models of contemporary country style – are to die for.

Higher West Hatch, Taunton, Somerset TA3 5RS Tel. 01823 480480, www.farmersinnwesthatch.co.uk Rooms available.

the garrick's head

After The King William did so well (*see* page 41) Charlie Digney and his wife Amanda extended their reach by opening this larger and grander pub in the centre of Bath. The approach is very much the same although there are different chefs in each kitchen. Sourcing is important and, as far as possible, whole animals, rather than cuts, are bought – and every bit is used. The food here could be said to be just slightly earthier than that at The King William – witness devilled kidneys on toast and cauliflower

cheese – and there are several dishes to share such as roast rib of beef with greens and anchovies. Admirably, 20 wines are served by the glass. Check out, too, the Digney's country pub, The Oakhill Inn in Oakhill, near Shepton Mallet.

7–8 St John's Place, Bath, Somerset, BA1 1ET Tel. 01225 318368, www.garricksheadpub.com Serves lunch every day and dinner (except Sunday).

the lord poulet arms

Fabulous. A perfectly kept 400 year-old inn in one of the prettiest villages in Somerset that manages to be both elegant and individual. The bar is refreshingly spare – no knick knacks, just flagstones and a huge fire. Good taste suffuses the place. The furniture is all antique oak or elm and the walls are in Farrow and Ball colours. The chef trained in Japan so there are a few oriental touches to the food, and these don't seem discordant as they are done with such a sure hand. But it's mostly modern British fare with much more interesting offerings than usual. Grilled Cornish sardines on toast, cumin and apple glazed pork belly, rhubarb and ginger beer 'soup' have all made their way onto the menu. There's a lavender edged boules piste outside, hammocks in the garden, homemade sloe gin and, in season, properly made Pimms. And – joy of joys – cider is served by the jug.

High Street, Hinton-St-George, Crewkerne, Somerset, TA17 8SE, Tel. 01460 73149, www.lordpoulettarms.com Serves lunch and dinner every day, rooms available.

the kensington arms

This place has sass. Its advertising catch-line (if they can be said to do anything as crass as promote themselves) is 'Just how your local should be', and indeed The Kensington Arms is the Brit-pub version of Cheers. It has a great vibe, is indefatigably youthful and cheery. Just check out their website and look also, at their country pub, The King's Arms in Litton, Somerset. The things which serious dining pubs usually eschew (quiz nights, the Grand Prix on a big screen) are here happily embraced. And chef Simon Bradley, who manned the stoves at the excellent Odettes in London, turns out terrific, vigorous food and puts together some great menus. Try girolle and parsley risotto with summer truffles, first class steak with béarnaise and hand-cut chips, or faggots with fresh peas and Guinness gravy.

There's a high-octane Saturday brunch as well with eggs Benedict (oh bliss) and a great fry-up. More locals should, indeed, be like this.

35–37 Stanley Road, Redland, Bristol, BS6 6NP
Tel. 0117 944 6444, www.thekensingtonarms.co.uk
Serves lunch every day and dinner (except Sunday).

the king william

A small pub on a busy road in one of the less pretty areas of Bath wouldn't seem to have a huge amount going for it, but people come from far and wide to eat Charlie Digney's food. This place can truly be said to be doing modern British cuisine, in that the ingredients are British – kale, mackerel, English cheeses, parsnips, asparagus, soft fruits. All this, rather than Mediterranean fare, is used here – and the dishes based on these ingredients are truly sympathetic to them, and to their locale. You might be offered ham hock with summer vegetables and boiled egg dressing, grilled sardines with roast beetroot and pickled blueberries or Montgomery cheddar tart with watercress and hazelnut salad. When eating at The King William, I thought that the British would be as famous as the French or the Italians are for their food, had this kind of cuisine developed in a more widespread way here. Which is quite an achievement on Digney's part.

36 Thomas Street, Bath, Somerset, BA1 5NN
Tel. 01225 428096, www.kingwilliampub.com
Serves lunch every day and dinner (except Sunday).

the queen's arms

Of all the couples now running a string of gastropubs (and there are quite a few), Londoners Rupert and Victoria Reeves are perhaps the best. They simply have flair, managing to make every place they take on somewhere you are delighted to spend time in, and all their places feel distinctive. The bar in this 18th-century stone pub must be one of my favourites anywhere – big tables, rug-strewn floors, a huge log-filled fire and soft chalky green walls. You can eat here or in the dining room – big mirrors, terra cotta walls – on locally sourced produce transformed into classy modern country food: nettle risotto, Dorset gammon with pineapple chutney, the pub's own eggs and fat chips, warm gooseberry tart with clotted Cornish cream. Other pubs might take a leaf out of their book when it comes to putting a menu together. Staff are young and utterly charming, and

the pub's labrador adds to the general chilled atmosphere. Check out their other place, The Stapleton Arms in Buckhorn Weston, too.

Corton Denham, Somerset, DT9 4LR, Tel. 01963 220317
www.thequeensarms.com
Serves lunch and dinner every day, rooms available.

the robin hood's retreat

This red-brick corner pub on one of Bristol's busiest roads has a chef – Nathan Muir – who has been making waves in the city. He used to work for Simon Hopkinson at Bibendum and is, like Hopkinson, not interested in the merely fashionable but in real food. It will take you ages to read the dishes on the large blackboard, and even longer to choose. There are a lot of solid sensible dishes which sound ordinary and comforting but which make a much bigger impression when they get to the table, simply because Muir is a perfectionist who wants to do the ordinary well. So even when it looks like you're just going to get roast chicken with sausage and bacon rolls, Nathan takes the dish into another league by pairing it with a silky cauliflower purée. There's a good balance between chunky food – terrines, slow braised brisket in stout – and lighter dishes such as sea bass with mustard butter. The interior is smart but not so done-up that it has driven away the drinkers (this is very much a drinker's as well as a diner's pub).

197 Gloucester Road, Bristol, BS7 8BG, Tel. 0117 924 8639
www.robinhoodsretreat.co.uk
Serves lunch (except Monday) and dinner (except Sunday).

the royal oak inn of luxborough

This is a deeply traditional place. Between September and February it is frequented by beaters and loaders and those generally enjoying the hunting season, and it's a haven if you're looking for a really old-fashioned country pub. There's a locals' bar with a warren of dining rooms off it (in great bright colours, one a deep blood-red, another bottle-green) all furnished with country furniture and checked curtains. Food is good, no-nonsense country cooking, done with flair. Dishes can be as simple as Cornish mussels with white wine or goat's cheese and courgette tart, or show originality, as with panfried cured salmon accompanied by celeriac mash and beetroot purée. As much of the food as possible is from the surrounding area – lamb and game, in particular, are terrific. An unusually authentic place, without airs and graces, this is a wonderful getaway for walkers (loads of books and maps are available) and those who just want some peace.

**Luxborough, Dunster, Somerset, TA23 0SH
Tel. 01984 640319, www.theroyaloakinnluxborough.co.uk
Serves lunch and dinner every day, rooms available.**

the wheelwright's arms

This grand old house, dating from the mid-18th century, was converted into a pub in 1981 and the present encumbents have totally refurbished it to make a tasteful, restrained space – perfect contemporary country. The food is a real mixture but works, nonetheless. There are quite a few trad English classics, along with Mediterranean favourites and unusual globally influenced dishes. Expect steak and kidney pie, dressed Devon crab, smoked haddock and gruyère fishcakes and Indian lamb with coconut sauce. Great sarnies, too.

**Church Lane, Monkton Combe, Bath, Somerset, BA2 7HB
Tel. 01225 722287, www.wheelwrightsarms.co.uk
Serves lunch and dinner every day, rooms available.**

the white hart inn

This is not the kind of place you just fall upon, and nothing about the outside, or its location (just a few minutes walk from Bath station), would make you think, 'oh, great place, must try it'. But friends lured me here and I'm not surprised it is now on the map with Bath foodies. Chef Rupert Pitt makes the kind of food that is popular in gastropubs – terrines, braised pork belly with a cider sauce, roast sea bass – and he is doing it so well. His food is fresh and intelligent, and this is a great place to hang out too – youthful, warm and fun.

**Widcombe Hill, Widcombe, Bath, Somerset, BA2 6AA
Tel. 01225 338053, www.whitehartbath.co.uk
Serves lunch and dinner every day.**

the bath arms

Chef-cum-landlord Dean Carr has cooked in some of the best-known restaurants in the country – Langan's Brasserie and The Ivy, to name but two – but he has always wanted to run and cook in a pub, and four years ago he took on this whitewashed pub on the Longleat Estate. He has maintained it as a pub – there are plenty of walkers and locals enjoying themselves – and the interior remains traditional, but he

also turns out some sound food. Old-fashioned pubby dishes, such as gammon with eggs and fish and chips are offered alongside more funky dishes, such as chicken with blue cheese fritters and rocket pesto, tomato terrine with Cornish crab mayo and chocolate brownie with malt ice-cream. A great place to know if you are visiting Longleat.

**Clay Street, Crockerton, Wiltshire, BA12 8AJ
Tel. 01985 212262, www.batharmscrockerton.co.uk
Serves lunch and dinner every day.**

the potting shed

An off-shoot of the smart boutique hotel, The Rectory (just 200 yards away), much is made of the pub's name in the décor. Trowels are used as door handles and there's even a light-fitting made out of a wheelbarrow. But it is not, heaven forbid, a theme pub. It's actually a beautiful interior, bright despite the low beams, with natural stone and whitewashed walls, tiled floors and a smattering of tongue and groove. And the menu is fab – full of classic British stuff. Pea and ham soup, baked egg with soldiers, slow-cooked shin of beef with mash, caramelized Dorset apple cake – it's a joy to read and to eat. A kitchen garden is being established to supply the pub with organic fruit, veg and herbs. Great British beers available, too.

**The Street, Crudwell, Malmesbury, Wiltshire, SN16 9EW
Tel. 01666 577833, www.thepottingshedpub.com
Serves lunch and dinner every day, rooms available
in the sister hotel up the road.**

the vine tree

A truly lovely place, this old watermill is everything a modern country pub should be. In the summer, it is flower bedecked and you can look at the Cotswolds from the terrace, glass in hand. In the winter, it is cosy and full of flickering candles glowing against deep red walls. Charles Walker and Tiggi Wood have created a feel-good space as well as a good eatery, and there's often an air of celebration about this pub. Food is classic simple stuff – asparagus with Hollandaise, Cotswold lamb with pea purée and mint, grilled sardines and Eton mess. Sunday lunch is great – local beef with all the trimmings – and children, grandparents and adults hanging out together.

**Foxley Road, Norton, Malmesbury, Wiltshire, SN16 0JP
Tel. 01666 837654, www.thevinetree.co.uk
Serves lunch and dinner every day.**

the south

Marlow is a frightfully well-heeled enclave on the Thames in Buckinghamshire. But it has been somewhat blighted by the usual chain shops and eateries and badly needed a distinctive eating place that wouldn't break the bank. In 2005, it arrived in the form of The Hand and Flowers. Owners Tom and Beth Kerridge (Tom cooks, Beth looks after just about everything else) have conjured an environment that is part pub, part country restaurant. Beth, an art college graduate, has created a warm, snug, tasteful space with bare brick walls, chunky tables and cushioned banquettes. Mirrors, vases of flowers and low-beamed ceilings make you want to hunker down and while-away the hours here. (In fact The Hand and Flowers gets a prize for the longest lunch I had while researching this book.)

Tom gained a Michelin star here after only 10 months. Talented is the chef who can turn out Michelin-starred food that actually works in a pub, and Tom has managed it. The menu is full of dishes – the signature braised shin of beef on parsnip purée, omelette Arnold Bennett, braised belly of pork with cauliflower purée and cockles, English asparagus with duck egg and morels – that are just the right side of complex for a pub but good enough to earn Michelin's accolades. He doesn't put too many flavours or textures on one plate, but there are real flashes you just don't expect, such as accompanying the braised shin of beef with carrots cooked with star anise, bringing a flavour and perfume which cuts through the richness of the meat. Intelligent food is no surprise when you learn Tom has spent his working life in some of the very best eateries in the country: City Rhodes, Odette's and Stephen Bull's in London and Adlard's in Norwich, where he managed to retain the restaurant's Michelin star.

Tom and Beth have also kept price at the front of their minds. They share the same desire to democratize eating out as many of the other owners featured in this book, and are well aware of how the Michelin star can frighten people off. Fish and chips are on at lunchtime, and they're happy for people to come in and have a bowl of soup instead of a three-course meal. And what soups you'll get: white bean with honey roast bacon and roast tomato with pesto, to name but two. They're proud of their well-kept ales as well.

The Kerridges have no interest in upping their game and trying to get two stars by opening a restaurant, but they do have great plans for running a small empire around the pub. They already have gorgeous cottages you can stay in and are in the process of building a small cookery school. With Tom's cooking and Beth's personality, The Hand and Flowers looks set to become one of the best-known dining pubs in the country.

the hand and flowers

126 WEST STREET, MARLOW, BUCKINGHAMSHIRE, SL7 2BP • TEL 01628 482277 • www.thehandandflowers.co.uk SERVES LUNCH (EVERY DAY) AND DINNER (MONDAY–SATURDAY), ROOMS AVAILABLE

makes 12 scotch eggs

FOR THE SCOTCH EGGS

50G (1¾OZ) MALDON SALT
50G (1¾OZ) CASTER SUGAR
1TSP SAFFRON
2TBSP PERNOD
4TBSP OLIVE OIL, PLUS EXTRA
TO COVER
2TBSP WHITE WINE
750G (1LB 10OZ) FRESH COD, (PIN-
BONED AND SKINNED)
4 BAKING POTATOES (ABOUT 300G/
10OZ IN WEIGHT ALTOGETHER)
2 CLOVES GARLIC, CRUSHED
12 QUAILS' EGGS
PLAIN FLOUR, 2 BEATEN EGGS AND
BREADCRUMBS, TO COAT

OIL FOR DEEP FRYING
12 SLICES CHORIZO SAUSAGE,
ABOUT 1CM (½ INCH) THICK

FOR THE RED PEPPER SAUCE

2TBSP OLIVE OIL
3 RED PEPPERS, SLICED
1 FRESH RED CHILLI, HALVED,
DESEEDED AND SLICED
2 SHALLOTS, CHOPPED
½TSP SAFFRON THREADS
50G (1¾OZ) CASTER SUGAR
50ML (2FL OZ) WHITE WINE VINEGAR
100ML (3½FL OZ) DRY WHITE WINE

salt cod scotch egg with red pepper sauce & chorizo

This is a great taste of Spain. And you don't have to source salt cod, just follow the instructions for how to do a light home-cure. Once you've tasted the sauce you'll make it for other dishes too – it's wonderful with roast Mediterranean fish.

Mix together the salt, sugar, saffron, Pernod, olive oil and white wine and pour the mix over the cod. Cover and leave for 24 hours in the fridge. To make the pepper sauce, heat the olive oil in a frying pan and sweat the peppers, chilli and shallots over a medium heat until soft. Add the saffron, sugar, vinegar and wine. Bring to the boil then turn down to a simmer and cook for 15 minutes. Blend and pass through a sieve. Set aside till you need it.

Preheat the oven to 140°C/275°F/gas mark 1. Rinse the cod under cold water to remove the marinade. Dry. Place the cod in a roasting tin where it fits snugly. Completely cover with olive oil. Put foil over the tin, place it in the oven and cook for about 20 minutes. Remove and leave to cool. Bake the potatoes until they are completely soft. Remove the skins and put the potato flesh through a sieve or potato ricer. Mix the cod with the potato and the garlic. Put the quails' eggs in boiling water for 2 minutes, take out and refresh in iced water. When they're cool, peel the shells off but be careful not to break the eggs. Shape the cod and potato mixture around the egg and form into a ball. Roll the balls in flour, then in the beaten egg and then in breadcrumbs. Heat oil to 180°C/350°F and deep-fry the balls for 2 minutes or until golden brown. Sauté or grill the slices of chorizo while the eggs are cooking. Heat the pepper sauce and serve the eggs with the chorizo and red pepper sauce.

'Talented is the chef who can turn out Michelin-starred food that actually works in a pub, and Tom has managed it. The menu is full of dishes – braised belly of pork with cauliflower purée and cockles, English asparagus with duck egg and morels – that are just the right side of complex.'

serves 6

500G (1LB 2OZ) SMOKED
   HADDOCK FILLET
10 EGGS
SALT AND PEPPER
50G (1¾OZ) LIGHTLY SALTED BUTTER
200G (7OZ) FRESHLY GRATED
   PARMESAN CHEESE
6 EGG YOLKS

FOR THE BÉCHAMEL SAUCE
600ML (1 PINT) MILK
2 CLOVES
2 BAY LEAVES

PARSLEY STALKS
1 ONION, ROUGHLY CHOPPED
30G (1OZ) BUTTER
30G (1OZ) FLOUR

FOR THE HOLLANDAISE
100ML (3½FL OZ) WHITE WINE
200ML (7FL OZ) WHITE WINE VINEGAR
4 BLACK PEPPERCORNS
A FEW TARRAGON STALKS
3 SHALLOTS, CHOPPED
2 EGG YOLKS
250G (9FL OZ) LIGHTLY SALTED BUTTER

smoked haddock omelette

At The Hand and Flowers they now cook individual omelettes in small blini pans but I divide the egg mixture between two frying pans.

First, start the béchamel. Put the milk, cloves, bay leaves, parsley stalks and onion into a pan and bring up to the boil. Remove from the heat and leave to infuse for 30 minutes or so. For the Hollandaise, put the white wine, white wine vinegar, black peppercorns, tarragon stalks and shallotts into a small saucepan and boil to reduce right down. Leave to cool.

Bring the milk back up to simmer and in it place the smoked haddock. Remove from the heat, cover and allow the fish to gently cook and then cool in the milk. Beat the 10 eggs and pass through a very fine sieve. Season. Take the haddock out of the milk and flake the fish. Sieve the milk mix into a saucepan and heat. In a separate pan, melt the 30g of butter, then add the flour and stir with a wooden spoon, mixing thoroughly. Keep on a medium heat until the mixture becomes straw coloured and the flour is cooked out – about 4 minutes. Take the pan off the heat and gradually whisk the milk into the roux. Season. Put the mixture back on the heat and, stirring all the time, bring it up to the boil to thicken. Simmer for 5 minutes, stirring occasionally. Now finish the Hollandaise sauce. Set a bowl over a pan of simmering water and in it blend the 2 egg yolks with the shallot reduction. Melt the 250g of butter and add slowly, whisking or stirring, adding more when the previous lot has been well incorporated and the mixture has thickened.

Melt the 50g of butter in two frying pans and divide the egg mixture between them. Cook the omelettes but keep them quite runny in the centre. Spoon the flaked haddock over each omelette and sprinkle with the Parmesan. Mix together 1 tbsp of béchamel with 1tbsp of the Hollandaise and one egg yolk per person. Spoon this mixture on top of the haddock. Glaze each omelette under a preheated grill until it is golden and bubbling. Serve immediately.

serves 4

1 LITRE (1¾ PINT) DUCK FAT
2 LAMB BREASTS
6 STAR ANISE
1 CINNAMON STICK
1 TBSP BLACK PEPPERCORNS
FLOUR AND OIL, FOR FRYING

FOR THE FAGGOTS
250G (9OZ) MINCED LAMB
50G (1¾OZ) LAMB'S LIVER, CHOPPED
1 EGG, BEATEN
50G (1¾OZ) FRESH WHITE
    BREADCRUMBS
10 SAGE LEAVES, CHOPPED

SALT AND PEPPER
250G (9OZ) CAUL FAT (ASK FOR THIS
    AT A BUTCHER'S)
CHICKEN STOCK, FOR POACHING

FOR THE LAMB SHANKS
4 LAMB SHANKS
2 CARROTS, DICED
1 CELERY STICK, DICED
1 ONION, ROUGHLY CHOPPED
1 HEAD OF GARLIC, HALVED (LEAVE
    SKIN ON)
1 BOTTLE GOOD RED WINE
2 LITRES (3½ PINTS) CHICKEN STOCK

braised shank of lamb with lamb faggots & crispy lamb breast

At The Hand and Flowers this is served with hispi cabbage and mashed potato.

Preheat the oven to 150°C/300°F/gas mark 2. Put the duck fat in a roasting tin and heat gently until melted. Put the breasts of lamb into this (the fat should cover the meat). Tie the spices together in a piece of muslin, add to the lamb and cover with tin foil. Cook in the oven for 3 hours and then leave the lamb to cool in the fat. When cool, remove the lamb, picking all the meat from the breast. Line a tray with nonstick baking paper and closely layer the meat on it. With a piece of baking paper on top, press with a heavy weight for 24 hours in the fridge.

To make the faggots, mix the mince, liver, egg, breadcrumbs and sage leaves and season well. Shape into balls and wrap in the caul fat. Leave these to rest in the fridge for 1 hour. Heat some oil in a frying pan and sear the faggots all over, then place them in hot chicken stock and poach for 25 minutes.

To braise the shanks, preheat the oven to 140°C/275°F/gas mark 1. Heat oil in a frying pan, add the shanks and brown them all over. Season. Remove and set aside. Brown the carrots, celery, onion and garlic in the same pan then put all the vegetables and the shanks into a large casserole dish. Cover with red wine and chicken stock and bring to the boil, then turn down to a simmer. Place a lid on the casserole and put in the oven for 2 hours. The lamb should be very tender and almost falling off the bone. Take the shanks out and keep them warm in a low oven. Sieve the cooking juices and boil them until you have a sauce-like consistency. Cut the lamb breast into 4 squares and dust lightly with flour. Heat some oil in a frying pan and fry the breast until crispy on both sides. Reheat the faggots in the stock and serve with the shanks and the breast of lamb.

serves 10

10 x 225G (8OZ) PIECES BEEF SHIN
1 GOOD BOTTLE OF RED WINE
150ML (¼ PINT) VEGETABLE OIL
1KG (2LB 4OZ) MIREPOIX (CARROTS,
  ONION AND CELERY CUT INTO
  2.5CM/1 INCH CHUNKS)
2 LITRES (3½ PINTS) VEAL STOCK (OR
  BEEF OR CHICKEN IF THAT'S EASIER)
10 BAY LEAVES
2 CLOVES
1TBSP WHITE PEPPERCORNS
BUNCH OF THYME
1 HEAD OF GARLIC, HALVED
  (LEAVE SKIN ON)

3TSP SALT
250G (9OZ) BUTTER, FOR SAUCE
10 x 2.5CM (1 INCH) LENGTHS
  OF MARROW BONE

FOR THE CARROTS
400ML (14FL OZ)WATER
250G (9OZ) BUTTER
150G (5½OZ) SUGAR
6 STAR ANISE
3TSP SALT
10 MEDIUM CARROTS (PEELED, TOPPED
  AND TAILED)

braised shin of beef with red wine

They also serve a dumpling and parsnip purée with this dish at The Hand and Flowers.

Marinate the shin of beef in the red wine for 24–48 hours. Remove and pat dry with kitchen paper. Preheat the oven to 170ºC/325ºF/gas mark 3. Bring the red wine used for the marinade to the boil and skim off the scum that rises to the top. In a large casserole dish, heat 75ml (2½fl oz) vegetable oil and sauté the mirepoix until browned. In a separate frying pan heat the remaining oil and sear the shins until well browned all over. Drain in a colander to get rid of any excess cooking fat.

Place the shins on top of the mirepoix and cover with the skimmed red wine and the stock. Add the bay leaves, cloves, white peppercorns, thyme, garlic and salt. Bring this up to a simmer and cover with a lid. Place in the oven and cook for 2½ hours.

To cook the carrots, bring the water, butter, sugar, star anise and salt to the boil in a pan. Add the carrots and cook until tender and the liquor has reduced by about half.

When the shins are cooked remove from the oven and leave to cool in the stock. Preheat the oven to 220ºC/425ºF/gas mark 7. Lift the shins from the stock and pass the stock through a fine sieve. Skim off any fat. Reduce by boiling, then pass through 6 layers of muslin cloth and leave to cool. To make the sauce reduce 500ml (18fl oz) of the shin stock and 250g (9oz) butter together until emulsified.

In a frying pan sear the bone marrow on both ends (no fat required) and place in the oven for 10 minutes or until the marrow is soft. To reheat the shin, warm it through in enough shin stock to just cover. Serve the shin, carrot and marrow in a bowl with some of the sauce spooned over.

serves 4

250ML (9FL OZ) RED WINE

350G (11½OZ) CASTER SUGAR

500G (1LB 2OZ) CHERRIES, PITTED

4 EGG YOLKS

2 EGGS

250ML (9FL OZ) DOUBLE CREAM

50ML (2FL OZ) KIRSCH

50G (1¾OZ) PLAIN FLOUR, SIFTED

15G (½OZ) FLAKED ALMONDS, TOASTED

ICING SUGAR, TO DUST

cherry clafoutis

Clafoutis, a French batter pudding, has enjoyed a bit of a renaissance of late and is very easy to make. This is a particularly lovely version.

Mix the wine and 250g (9oz) sugar in a saucepan and gently bring to the boil, stirring to help the sugar dissolve. Pour over the pitted cherries. Leave to cool. Preheat the oven to 170°C/325°F/gas mark 3.

Whisk the yolks, eggs and remaining 100g (3½oz) sugar together. Add the cream and the Kirsch and gently fold in the flour. The mixture should have the consistency of a Yorkshire pudding batter.

Scoop the cherries out of the sweetened wine with a slotted spoon and put them into a gratin dish or individual ramekins. Pour on the clafoutis mix and bake for 15–20 minutes. Scatter toasted flaked almonds on top and dust with icing sugar. Serve immediately.

You get a real thrill walking into Baughurst's Wellington Arms. It's tiny – only eight tables – and the busyness and passion emanating from the kitchen hits you immediately. Owners Simon Page, who does front-of-house, and Jason King, who cooks, are like a couple of kids who've found themselves running their own sweet shop. They love what they do and their enthusiasm is infectious. They're not amateurs, though – far from it. Jason is an Ozzie who worked in the best places in Melbourne before meeting Simon in Hong Kong.

They decided to relocate here to Britain and ran a catering company before taking on the pub in 2005 on the sort of mad whim that marks some of the best dining pubs and makes them so truly individual. Opening a restaurant didn't appeal. 'We couldn't have afforded it,' says Jason. 'We had enough to buy a short lease from the brewery and that was all. But I didn't want a restaurant anyway. That smacks of a glass-fronted box on a high street. We wanted a place where you could come in your wellingtons if you felt like it, where we could create the kind of space we wanted and cook the kind of food we liked without any rules. The pub is so small and such a personal kind of place that we do sometimes feel as if we've opened up our living room to people,' he says with a grin.

The tables and chairs – all Edwardian and as carefully sourced as the food – make you feel as if you're at your granny's, except that granny never paid this much attention to detail: twinkling tealights of amber glass (lit even during the day in the colder months), linen blinds, perfect pats of butter and neat salt and pepper holders. As you read the blackboard menu you are cocooned in homeliness: jars of honey from the pub's own bees, homemade jams and chutneys and teapots with cosies knitted by Simon's mum line the bar, and there are boxes of eggs from their own chickens on the counter, all for sale.

The food is a mixture of British fare (despite being from Oz, Jason is a stickler for running an English venture and using local produce) with a few splashes of exotic colour and some original spins on better-known dishes. You might find potted local trout with homemade pickles and toast soldiers, venison and field mushrooms in red wine with rosemary dumplings, free-range pork with homemade apple jelly, Moroccan chicken stew and candied quince and almond tart. Rural, home-grown and local is written all over it. This is honest food, beautifully executed.

With their own chickens, bees, fruit trees and vegetables out at the back, Jason and Simon are doing what many people dream about but never pursue. Thank goodness they're allowing us into their living room.

the wellington arms

BAUGHURST ROAD, BAUGHURST, HAMPSHIRE, RG26 5LP • TEL 0118 982 0110 • www.thewellingtonarms.com
SERVES LUNCH (EXCEPT MONDAY AND TUESDAY) AND DINNER (EXCEPT SUNDAY AND MONDAY)

serves 4

2 LARGE BROWN TROUT

50G (1¾OZ) SEA SALT

200G (7OZ) LARGE LEAFED LOOSE TEA
(SUCH AS ASSAM)

200G (7OZ) PLAIN RICE

300G (10OZ) UNSALTED BUTTER

2 CLOVES GARLIC, VERY
FINELY SLICED

500G (1LB 2OZ) SAMPHIRE

50G (1¾OZ) TINY CAPERS, RINSED
OF SALT OR BRINE

JUICE OF ¼ LEMON

4 VERY FRESH FREE-RANGE EGGS

tea smoked brown trout on samphire with poached egg & brown butter

Jason and Simon are lucky enough to get a lot of home-grown ingredients brought to their kitchen door by customers. Jason writes, 'One day a young man called Dan arrived offering to catch fish for us. He was so enthusiastic we took him up on his offer, not really expecting to see him often. However that same weekend he turned up with 10 fat rainbow trout, 4 brown trout and a bucket of live crayfish. And so began a need to find new and interesting ways of using trout. This is one.'

Get your fishmonger to fillet and pin-bone the trout. Rub the flesh with sea salt and leave to cure for 15 minutes. Wash off the salt. Line an old roasting tin with foil and sprinkle in the tea and rice. Place a cake rack or a grill rack in the tin and put the fish on top, skin-side down. Set the roasting tin on the stove and heat until smoking. Cover the entire tin with tin foil and cook for 2 minutes. Remove the foil and inspect the fish. It should still be quite raw, but smell lightly smoky. Refrigerate the fish until needed.

Preheat the oven to 180°C/350°F/gas mark 4. For the samphire, bring a large pan of water to the boil. Melt one third of the butter in a frying pan, add the garlic and fry until crispy (but not dark brown – it burns quickly so take care). Plunge the samphire into the boiling water for a few seconds. Remove, drain immediately and add to the butter in the pan. Toss to get coated in the garlic. Melt the remaining butter in a small frying pan. Add the capers and cook until the capers become crisp and the butter begins to brown. Add lemon juice and cover to keep warm.

Place the smoked trout fillets on a baking sheet lined with nonstick baking paper and bake for 6–8 minutes. Take care to serve the trout medium to medium rare. For the poached eggs, bring a small pan of water to the boil. Create a vortex in the centre of the pan by stirring rapidly with a large spoon. Crack the eggs one at a time into the centre as it continues to spin. Simmer for 2 minutes or so depending on how runny you like your eggs. To serve, arrange the samphire on plates and top each portion with a poached egg. Lay a fish fillet beside and spoon over the butter sauce. Can be served with new potatoes.

serves 6

250G (9OZ) RICOTTA CHEESE
150G (5½OZ) PARMESAN CHEESE,
   GRATED
PINCH OF FRESHLY GRATED NUTMEG
PINCH OF CAYENNE PEPPER
FINELY GRATED RIND OF ½ LEMON
SALT AND PEPPER
12 PUMPKIN OR COURGETTE FLOWERS
VEGETABLE OIL, FOR FRYING

FOR THE BATTER
300G (10½OZ) SELF-RAISING FLOUR
150–200ML (5–7FL OZ) REAL ALE
SEA SALT

FOR THE LEMON DRESSING
JUICE OF 1 LEMON
2TBSP OF RUNNY HONEY
250ML (9FL OZ) EXTRA VIRGIN
   OLIVE OIL
SALT AND PEPPER

GREEN LEAVES, SUCH AS WATERCRESS,
   ROCKET, LAMB'S LETTUCE OR
   BABY SPINACH
SHAVED PARMESAN CHEESE, TO SERVE

crispy fried pumpkin flowers stuffed with ricotta & parmesan

At The Wellington Arms, they grow a variety of squashes through the summer. The plants produce a surplus of male flowers (the ones that don't produce the squash) and it is these flowers that they pick each morning to make dishes such as this fantasic entrée. You can also order courgette flowers from your greengrocer but these are generally expensive and flown in from Italy, and it is recommended that you grow your own. The plants themselves don't require much care other than water and fertile soil or a growbag.

Combine both the cheeses, the spices and the lemon rind together using a fork and season to tatse. Remove the stamens from the flower centres. (The stamens are very bitter, and have to be removed. No short cuts!) Use a teaspoon to fill the flower cavities with the cheese mixture. Twist the tips of the flower petals together to seal the flower and refrigerate until you want to cook them.

Using a hand whisk, mix the beer into the self-raising flour along with a pinch of salt. The batter should have the consistency of thick double cream. Add more beer if you need to. To make the lemon dressing just combine all the ingredients in a jam jar and shake vigorously.

Heat the vegetable oil in a deep saucepan to 180°C/350°F. Dip the individual flowers in the beer batter and gently shake off the excess. Deep-fry the flowers in small batches until light golden brown. Put them on to kitchen paper to absorb the excess oil. Serve with a leaf salad tossed with the lemon dressing and a little shaved Parmesan.

serves 10

200G (7OZ) MINCED SHOULDER OR
  LEG OF VENISON
1 RABBIT, FLESH MINCED
1 PHEASANT, FLESH MINCED
300G (10½OZ) PORK BELLY, MINCED
150G (5½OZ) PORK FAT, MINCED
1 CAN DUCK FAT (200ML WHEN
  LIQUID)
3 JUNIPER BERRIES, CRUSHED

LEAVES FROM 2 SPRIGS OF THYME
2 CLOVES GARLIC, FINELY CHOPPED
PINCH OF MACE
2TSP SEA SALT
1½TSP PEPPER
20 THIN SLICES PANCETTA
4 BAY LEAVES
OLIVE OIL, TOAST AND CHUTNEY, TO SERVE

game terrine of local venison, rabbit & pheasant

Your terrine will taste better over time, so remember to make it a few days in advance. You can ask your butcher to bone and coarsely mince all the game for you.

At the pub, they confit the livers and hearts from the rabbit and pheasant (and the rabbit's kidneys) and put them into the terrine whole to create an interesting cross section when the terrine is sliced and served. Alternatively, you could mince them into the mix. To confit the offal, salt the livers, hearts and kidneys overnight – just sprinkle on all sides with salt and put into the fridge. Next morning wash off the salt and warm the duck fat in a saucepan. Add the offal and cover with tin foil, then cook in an oven preheated to 170°C/325°F/gas mark 3 until tender (about 40 minutes).

Mix the minced meats and fat together with the crushed juniper berries, thyme, garlic, mace, salt and pepper. Cover with clingfilm and allow the mixture to infuse overnight in the fridge. It's a good idea to fry a little of the mixture to see whether it is well enough seasoned – terrines need good seasoning. Preheat the oven to 170°C/325°F/gas mark 3. Line a terrine mould with foil, triple-folded for strength, with extra overhang to allow you to remove the terrine in one piece when it's cold. Lay the pancetta into the terrine mould, allowing plenty to overhang down the sides. Press the mince firmly into the mould to ensure a smooth shape. Add the confit offal randomly if you are using it that way. Top with bay leaves and cover with the overhanging pancetta. Cover the top of the terrine mould with foil. Put the terrine into a roasting tin and fill the tin with boiling water. Bake for about 2 hours.

When the terrine is cooked (a metal skewer inserted in the middle should come out hot) remove from the water bath and leave to cool slightly. About 1 hour later, place a heavy object on top of the terrine to press it down. Jason uses an old house brick covered in tin foil and clingfilm. To serve, remove the terrine from the mould using the foil handles and carefully peel off the foil, trying to retain the jelly around the terrine. Cut into thick slices (1–2 cm/½inch each). Dribble a little olive oil on to the surface of the terrine (to enhance the colour and make it shiny) and finish with a fresh grind of black pepper. Serve with hot toast and chutney.

serves 6

6 GREY-LEG OR RED-LEG PARTRIDGES,
    PLUCKED AND TRUSSED
6 SPRIGS OF ROSEMARY
6 BAY LEAVES
6 SPRIGS OF THYME
OIL
SALT AND VINEGAR
200ML (7FL OZ) WHITE WINE
200ML (7FL OZ) GAME, VEAL OR
    STRONG CHICKEN STOCK

FOR THE RED CABBAGE
1 RED CABBAGE, ABOUT 2KG (4LB 8OZ)
500G (1LB 2OZ) RED ONIONS
35G (1¼OZ) BUTTER

JUICE OF 1 LEMON
300G (10½OZ) STEWED DAMSONS
300ML (½ PINT) RED WINE
100G (3½OZ) SOFT DARK BROWN SUGAR
50ML (2FL OZ) RED WINE VINEGAR
50ML (2FL OZ) BALSAMIC VINEGAR
1 CINNAMON STICK
1 BAY LEAF
2.5CM (1 INCH) SQUARE FRESH ROOT
    GINGER, PEELED AND FINELY GRATED

FOR THE PARSNIP CHIPS
3 PARSNIPS
OIL, FOR FRYING
SEA SALT

whole roast partridge stuffed with sage & rosemary on sticky red cabbage & parsnip chips

Jason says, 'The cabbage in this dish needs to be soft but not a pulp. You may need to cook the cabbage for more or less time than suggested, depending on how fresh your cabbage is. Our cabbages, which we grow ourselves, need very little cooking as they are picked when we need them.'

Thinly slice the cabbage and red onions. In a large saucepan, sauté the red onions in the butter until soft. Add the lemon juice and stir well. Add the cabbage, cover with a lid and cook for 5 minutes over a moderate heat. Put all the remaining ingredients for the cabbage into the pan, cover and cook for a further 40 minutes on a low heat, stirring occasionally. Braised red cabbage will keep for up to 1 week covered well in the fridge.

For the partridge, preheat the oven to its very highest setting. Stuff the partridge cavities with the herbs. Oil and season the birds and put them in a roasting tin. Roast for 12 minutes if you are cooking English grey-leg partridge, 16 minutes if you are cooking red-leg ones. Rest the birds for 8 minutes – cover in foil and insulate them with tea towels – before serving. Deglaze the pan with the white wine. Reduce the liquid by half then add the stock, bring to the boil, pass through a fine sieve and keep warm. Reheat the cabbage. To make the chips, shave the parsnips into long strips with a potato peeler until you've used up all the flesh. Fry the shavings in small batches in a saucepan of oil heated to 180°C/350°F. Place the freshly fried shavings on kitchen paper (to soak up excess fat) and season with sea salt. Put some hot red cabbage on plates, top with the partridges and finish with parsnip chips. Serve with a little jug of sauce.

www.thewellingtonarms.com

Telephone: 0118 982 0110

'We wanted a place in the countryside and we came to see The Wellington Arms. There was someone in riding boots having a drink and a dog lying by the bar and we just thought, this is it.'

serves 10

FOR THE SHORTBREAD

115G (4OZ) CASTER SUGAR

250G (9OZ) BUTTER, AT ROOM TEMPERATURE

235G (8OZ) PLAIN FLOUR

115G (4OZ) CORNFLOUR

100G (3½OZ) CRYSTALLIZED STEM GINGER, VERY FINELY CHOPPED

300G (10½OZ) SUGAR

1 CINNAMON STICK

150ML (¼ PINT) WATER

1KG (2LB 4OZ) DAMSONS, STONED (OR NOT)

CORNISH CLOTTED CREAM, TO SERVE

stem ginger shortbread with damsons & cornish clotted cream

Miraculously Simon and Jason manage to get the stones out of their damsons without too much trouble, but in most damon varieties the flesh clings really firmly to the stones. If you can't remove the stones then leave them in, but warn your guests. This is a country sort of dish so there's nothing wrong with serving it in this way.

To make the shortbread, preheat the oven to 150°C/300°F/gas mark 2. Beat the sugar and butter together with an electric mixer for about 15 minutes until creamy. Sift the flour and cornflour together and stir into the butter and sugar mix. Add the ginger. Tip on to a very lightly floured worktop and knead lightly to form a soft dough.

Line a baking sheet with nonstick baking paper. Press the dough gently onto the sheet, keeping the surface even. Bake for 10 minutes then cut lines into the dough to form squares and return the shortbread to the oven, baking for a further 5–10 minutes or until light brown in colour. Dust the shortbread with caster sugar while still warm. Leave to firm up and cool before removing from the baking sheet.

To stew the damsons, heat the sugar, cinnamon and water together until the soft boil is reached (118°C on a sugar thermometer). Add the damsons, cover and cook until soft. Serve the damsons warm, at room temperature or chilled, with the shortbread and plenty of clotted cream.

serves 10

250G (9OZ) BUTTER, AT ROOM TEMPERATURE,
  PLUS EXTRA FOR GREASING
10TBSP HONEY, PLUS MORE FOR DRIZZLING
10 DESSERT APPLES, PEELED AND STEWED WITH
  A LITTLE SUGAR TO TASTE
250G (9OZ) CASTER SUGAR
3 FREE-RANGE EGGS, LIGHTLY BEATEN
250G (9OZ) SELF-RAISING FLOUR
FINELY GRATED RIND OF 1 LEMON

FOR THE CUSTARD
500ML (18FL OZ) FULL FAT MILK
400ML (14FL OZ) DOUBLE CREAM
1 BAY LEAF
1 CLOVE
1 BROAD STRIP OF ORANGE RIND, WITH PITH
  REMOVED
9 FREE-RANGE EGG YOLKS
50G (1¾OZ) CASTER SUGAR

steamed apple & wellington honey sponge pudding with proper custard

Chef Jason makes the custard for this with eggs from the Wellington's own chickens and honey from their bees. You can cook the puddings in advance and reheat them.

Preheat the oven to 150°C/300°F/gas mark 2. Butter 10 pudding moulds, each with a 250ml (9fl oz) capacity. Spoon 1tbsp of honey into each mould and cover with stewed apple. To make the sponge, beat the butter and sugar together until creamy, using an electric mixer. Add the eggs a little at a time then fold in the flour and the lemon rind. Spoon into the prepared moulds and set the moulds into a roasting tin. Pour in boiling water to come halfway up the sides of the moulds and bake for 20 minutes.

For the custard, heat the milk, cream, bay leaf, clove and orange peel together until just boiling. Remove from the heat, cover the pan with clingfilm and leave to infuse for at least 20 minutes. Strain to remove the flavourings. Beat the egg yolks and sugar together until really thick and slightly pale. Add one-third of the milk mixture to the egg mixture and whisk in thoroughly. Add the remaining milk and strain through a fine sieve. Return to the stove top in a clean pan and cook over a low heat, stirring continuously – do not let it boil or the eggs will scramble – until the sauce coats the back of a spoon. Remove from the heat. Unmould the puddings onto plates and drizzle with a bit of honey. Serve with the warm custard.

Rather good English wines

the best of the rest

the plough

In a lovely old building (its origins date from the 1400s) painstakingly and beautifully restored after a fire 15 years ago, chef-proprietor Martin Lee is turning out great dishes – English, French and Italian – which are unfussy but intelligently wrought. A devil for provenance and quality, he seems to spend as much time sourcing his food as cooking it. The more English dishes are mouth-wateringly old-fashioned (try homemade black pudding and smoked bacon with Montgomery Cheddar hash) and the Mediterranean dishes too are real, not gussied up. You might find slow cooked shoulder of lamb with chickpeas or potato gnocchi with roast courgettes. There's also a welcome section on the menu entitled 'simple dishes': a selection of faves which have become gastropub classics. From this you can choose a mean steak sandwich or tip-top fish and chips with pease pudding. It is one of the best places in the book for Sunday lunch, too.
Kimbolton Road, Bolnhurst, St Neots, Bedfordshire MK44 2EX, Tel. 01234 376274, www.bolnhurst.com
Serves lunch (except Monday) and dinner (except Sunday and Monday).

the greene oak

Henry and Catherine Cripps, the couple behind The Greene Oak, ran gastropubs in London and have brought great panache to this, their own venture. The menu is a rundown of the classics we Brits like to dine on when eating out informally these days, such as Caesar salad, sausages with bubble and squeak and fish cakes with tomato and caper sauce. And all is cooked with admirable skill. It's a charming place, too, decked out in a relaxing soft green with big chunky mirrors and antique light fittings. There is a well-judged blend of old and contemporary with service as delightful as the décor and food.
Oakley Green, Windsor, Berkshire, SL4 5UW Tel. 01753 864294, www.thegreeneoak.co.uk
Serves lunch every day and dinner (except Sunday).

the hind's head

If you watched any of Heston Blumenthal's television programmes you'll have seen him running between his kitchen at The Fat Duck (his famous gaff up the road) and this pub, which he bought in 2004. The food for which he is well known – the chemistry lab stuff that has made snail porridge famous, even among non-foodies – is not what you get here but it's equally worthy of adulation. Earthy and old-fashioned – Heston undertook research on old local dishes before he put the menu together – every single dish is finely tuned. Potted shrimps, oxtail and kidney pudding, rabbit and bacon terrine with cucumber pickles. Even the Scotch eggs and devils on horseback are perfection. It also happens to be a lovely, proper pub, with ancient beams and glowing fires. Although the dining experience here is very different from the one you'll get at The Fat Duck, it's still a good way to taste Heston's food without taking out a mortgage.
High Street, Bray, Maidenhead, Berkshire, SL6 2AB Tel. 01628 626151, www.hindsheadhotel.co.uk
Serves lunch every day and dinner (except Sunday).

the pot kiln

After buying this idyllic, red brick ale-house, chef-owner Mike Robinson gave the interior a lick of paint and opened for business. It is, apparently, where he had his first pint. He has been cooking terrific country fare ever since he took over. The menu is strong in old-fashioned English dishes – mutton and suet pudding, Cornish pasties and game pie, for example – but there are great platefuls of French and Italian food, too, and some which blend influences from all three, such as confit of belly pork with cavolo nero, puréed white beans and cider and thyme gravy. The bar is tiny and totally unreconstructed (darts-playing locals fill it up quickly) and the place is nicely tucked away.
Frilsham, Yattendon, Berkshire, RG18 0XX Tel. 01635 201366, www.potkiln.co.uk
Serves lunch and dinner every day.

the royal oak

This place, owned by Michael Parkinson and his son, Nick, has enjoyed rave reviews since it opened, and no wonder. Dominic Chapman, a former chef at Heston Blumenthal's sterling establishment, The Hind's Head, is in charge of the kitchen and he has a gift for gilding and reinvigorating old English classics. And what classics are those? Macaroni cheese with ham hock, salt-beef stovey with a fried egg and mustard sauce, lemon sole with cucumber and brown shrimps. His Scotch eggs – tender sausage meat encasing a soft quail's egg – are worth the journey alone. The décor is lovely too – soft and warm and properly pubby with beams et al. Terrific stuff.

**Paley Street, Maidenhead, Berkshire, SL6 3JN
Tel. 01628 620541, www.theroyaloakpaleystreet.com
Serves lunch every day and dinner (except Sunday).**

the old queen's head

The Salisburys, who opened their first gastropub, The Alford Arms, in Frithsden in Hertfordshire, now have The Old Queen's Head in Penn plus The Swan in Denham and The Royal Oak in Marlow (all in Buckinghamshire) and every one is excellent (the web address below will direct you to the other pubs). The Queen's Head follows the same formula as the others, without being formulaic. The menu is full of gastropub classics and more innovative dishes. You might find oak-smoked bacon with bubble and squeak, poached egg and Hollandaise sauce, salmon steak on a broad bean boxty cake with chervil butter, or pizza with manchego cheese, roast tomatoes, wild garlic and asparagus. Like the other pubs in the group, the inside is stylish but still pubby with its colour-washed walls, glowing wooden floors and warming rugs.

**Hammersley Lane, Penn, High Wycombe,
Buckinghamshire, HP10 8EY
Tel. 01494 813371, www.oldqueensheadpenn.co.uk
Serves lunch and dinner every day.**

the three horseshoes inn

After a decade in London restaurants – Le Gavroche, The Connaught and Chez Nico – chef-patron Simon Crawshaw decided to follow the path of many young, talented cooks and take his family out of the big smoke and to a bucolic part of the country. Lucky for the denizens of the Chilterns that he did, for here is elegant, well-judged food: seared scallops with chorizo and cauliflower, lamb rump with aubergine purée and black olive jus and a cracking lemon posset with raspberries. There are also terrific sarnies on offer. The bar is small and perfectly formed, or you can eat in the dining room. Lovely bedrooms upstairs too, all done up in Farrow and Ball and bold, expensive fabrics.

**Horseshoe Road, Bennett End, Radnage, High Wycombe,
Buckinghamshire, HP14 4EB, Tel. 01494 483273
www.thethreehorseshoes.net
Serves lunch and dinner every day (but closes Sunday
at 8pm) rooms available.**

the fox and hounds

Chef-owner James Rix used to be at the helm at The Cow, the fashionable Notting Hill gastropub. It's great for the denizens of Hertfordshire that he has opened this, his own gaff, and is doing even better food than before. The menu is mostly a mixture of French, Spanish and Italian dishes but they are still all recognizably 'James Rix'; he brings his own touches to dishes and cooks and sources intelligently and carefully. Temptations include pasta rotolo with cavolo nero, chestnuts and mushrooms (he is particularly strong on Italian stuff), skate wing with ratte potatoes, salsa verde and walnuts, or squid, chorizo and white bean stew. The place has a cool vibe – you immediately know it's run by a young chef who's come straight from somewhere hip: there are soft leather sofas in the bar and the dining room has a delightful shabby chic appeal.

**2 High Street, Hunsdon, Hertfordshire, SG12 8NH
Tel. 01279 843999, www.foxandhounds-hunsdon.co.uk
Serves lunch (except Monday) and dinner (except
Sunday and Monday).**

london

Stroll by this pub on a busy shopping street in Dulwich and you won't be able to stop yourself going in. Some of the tables are kept permanently ready for diners and the glistening wine glasses in the wood-panelled rooms look irresistible. If you're passing mid-morning it's a great place to hunker down with a coffee and the paper (they have all the dailies). In winter, they light the fires at about 11am and the crackle and smell of burning logs and the gentle buzz of pre-lunch activity makes it the perfect place just to hang out. And then, of course, it's time for lunch, and The Palmerston gets even better.

Chef and owner Jamie Younger worked at Simon Hopkinson's gaff, Bibendum, along with such stalwarts as Jeremy Lee and Bruce Poole, and by eating at The Palmerston you get the advantages not just of his training but also of his sourcing. Jamie still buys from the same people he dealt with before, which means that the steak au poivre you eat at The Palmerston (Galloway beef, hung for 32 days) is as good, and cheaper, than you'd get at Bibendum.

Jamie's food has the feel of Hopkinson's, and of Rowley Leigh's. The menu is so full of modern classics (plus a few revamped British dishes) that the only difficulty is making choices. You might find vincisgrassi, the 18th-century Italian dish – basically a lasagne made with wild mushrooms, Parma ham and truffles – made famous by Franco Taruschio at The Walnut Tree Inn, or a salad of bacon and smoked eel (the latter is a favourite ingredient and appears in different guises). And then there's the stuff that you would only normally find in a classy restaurant, such as Muscat-marinated ballotine of foie gras, scrambled eggs with white Alba truffles, or halibut with girolles, samphire and lobster sauce. But somehow these dishes, delivered on plain white plates with no fancy-pants presentation, don't feel out of place. It just seems like great food delivered without fuss.

Jamie visits all the farms from where he sources his meat. The fish comes from Dorset every day, and leaves and herbs come from the redoubtable Secretts in Kent. Specialist Spanish and Italian suppliers provide the considerable amount of chorizo, Cantabrian anchovies, Castelluccio lentils and cotechino sausage that get used.

The Palmerston came about because Jamie lived nearby and wanted somewhere to go for a good Sunday lunch with his mates, or where he could get a pint and a plate of good food midweek. The Palmerston is always humming, but it has managed to remain chicly shabby even as the area gets smarter. There are as many louche media freelancers at the bar of an evening as there are well-heeled couples at the dining tables. It's got a great feel, this place. I wish Jamie would move to my area.

the palmerston

91 LORDSHIP LANE, LONDON, SE22 8EP • TEL 020 8693 1629 • www.thepalmerston.net
SERVES LUNCH AND DINNER EVERY DAY (EXCEPT SUNDAY DINNER)

serves 4

250G (9OZ) RATTE POTATOES (OR OTHER WAXY
    VARIETY OF POTATO)
500G (1LB 2OZ) CEPS, WIPED CLEAN WITH A
    DAMP CLOTH
4–6TBSP EXTRA VIRGIN OLIVE OIL
100G (3½OZ) BUTTER
6 CLOVES GARLIC, FINELY CHOPPED
SALT AND PEPPER
JUICE OF ½ LEMON
SMALL BUNCH FLAT-LEAF PARSLEY,
    COARSELY CHOPPED
4 FREE-RANGE EGGS

sautéed ceps and potatoes with garlic, parsley & fried egg

A great lunch or supper dish. If your purse can't stretch to ceps use cultivated mushrooms, or a mixture of cultivated and wild ones.

Place the potatoes in salted cold water and bring to the boil. Cook until just tender. Halve the potatoes or cut the larger ones into chunks. Slice the ceps 5mm (¼ inch) thick. Heat 3tbsp oil in a large cast-iron frying pan and add the ceps, three-quarters of the butter and the potatoes, and cook until golden brown. Add the garlic, salt and pepper, and toss together. Remove from the heat and add the lemon juice and chopped parsley.

In a separate pan, fry the eggs (without browning them), in a little olive oil and the remaining butter. Season to taste. Divide the ceps and potato mixture between 4 plates, place an egg on top of each portion, drizzle with olive oil and serve.

serves 4

4 SLICES A-GRADE FOIE GRAS (1CM/½ INCH THICK)	SALT AND PEPPER
250G (9OZ) SMOOTH MASHED POTATOES	25ML (1FL OZ) DRY WHITE WINE
2 EGG WHITES	100ML (3½FL OZ) STRONG CHICKEN STOCK
2 WHOLE EGGS	A FEW DROPS OF CHARDONNAY VINEGAR
1TBSP PLAIN FLOUR	VEGETABLE OIL
2TBSP MILK	4 BLACK FIGS
2TBSP DOUBLE CREAM	A LITTLE CASTER SUGAR

sautéed foie gras with potato pancakes, grilled figs & chardonnay vinegar sauce

This is an unquestionably luxurious dish but it's very easy to make. One to stun guests with.

Take the foie gras out of the fridge and let it warm to room temperature. For the pancake mix, mix together the potatoes, egg whites, whole eggs, flour, milk, double cream and salt and pepper to taste, until smooth. To make the sauce, reduce the white wine by boiling until there's only a couple of teaspoons left, then add the stock and reduce further to a sauce-like consistency. Add a few drops of chardonnay vinegar to taste.

Heat some vegetable oil in a nonstick frying pan. Make the pancakes by frying spoonfuls of the potato mixture until golden brown on both sides. Put in a low oven to keep warm.

Halve the figs, brush with oil and sprinkle a little caster sugar on the cut side. Grill the figs in a ridged frying pan until caramelized, moving them around so they get the customary cross-hatching marks.

Heat a heavy, cast-iron frying pan until very hot. Season the slices of foie gras and place in the pan (you do not need oil as the foie gras contains enough fat for cooking). Cook on one side until golden brown, then turn over and remove from the heat. The foie gras will continue to cook in the pan for a couple of minutes while you prepare the plates.

Place one pancake on each of 4 plates with the foie gras on top and then a fig on top of that. Dress with the sauce and serve.

fillet of wild salmon with lemon, dill & broad bean butter sauce

Simple and elegant, with the taste of early summer.

serves 4

100ML (3½FL OZ) LEMON JUICE

1 BANANA SHALLOT, FINELY CHOPPED

2TBSP DOUBLE CREAM

175G (6OZ) COLD UNSALTED BUTTER, DICED, FOR THE SAUCE, PLUS 25G (1OZ) SLAB FOR FRYING

SALT AND PEPPER

1TBSP VEGETABLE OIL

4 SALMON FILLETS, 180G (6OZ) EACH

100G (3½OZ) COOKED AND SKINNED BROAD BEANS

2TBSP CHOPPED DILL

Preheat the oven to 180°C/350°F/gas mark 4. Put the lemon juice and shallot in a pan and boil to reduce until almost gone, then add the cream and bring to the boil again. Whisk in the diced butter piece by piece and season.

Heat the remaining slab of butter and the vegetable oil in a nonstick ovenproof frying pan and colour the salmon on both sides. Put in the oven and bake for 4 minutes. Take the pan out of the oven, turn the salmon over and let it rest in the pan.

Gently reheat the butter sauce (it must not boil) and add the broad beans and dill. Divide between 4 warmed plates, place the salmon on top and serve.

breadcrumbed escalopes of english pink veal with prosciutto, fontina & sage

This is typical of the old-fashioned but classic dishes Jamie turns out at The Palmerston. It's a great one to have up your sleeve.

serves 4

4 VEAL ESCALOPES

4 SLICES PROSCIUTTO

SMALL BUNCH OF SAGE

100G (3½OZ) FONTINA CHEESE

50G (1¾OZ) PLAIN FLOUR

2 EGGS, BEATEN

100G (3½OZ) WHITE BREADCRUMBS

6TBSP VEGETABLE OIL

100G (3½OZ) UNSALTED BUTTER

SALT AND PEPPER

1 LEMON

Wrap each escalope in clingfilm and bash until wafer thin, making sure you do not make any holes or tear the meat. Lay them out and on each one place a slice of prosciutto, 3 sage leaves and a slice of fontina. Fold the meat over and pinch the edges together.

Dip the veal in flour, then the beaten eggs, and finally the breadcrumbs. Heat the oil in a frying pan, add the butter, season the veal and fry over a moderate heat until golden brown. Turn over, and repeat on the other side. Remove the meat from the pan and rest. Add the remaining sage leaves to the pan and fry until crisp (be careful not to let the butter burn). Place the veal on warmed plates with the crispy sage leaves on top. If the butter in the pan hasn't burnt, pour over the meat. If it has burnt, melt another 75g (3oz) and use instead. Serve with sautéed potatoes, a green salad and a wedge of lemon.

serves 4

FOR THE JELLY
4 BLOOD ORANGES
250ML (9FL OZ) CHAMPAGNE
100ML (3½FL OZ) SUGAR SYRUP
  (DISSOLVE 50G/1¾OZ SUGAR IN
  50ML/2FL OZ BOILING WATER)
5 LEAVES GELATINE

FOR THE MADELEINES
85G (3OZ) BROWN SUGAR
2 EGGS

30G (1OZ) HONEY
85G (3OZ) BUTTER
85G (3OZ) PLAIN FLOUR
3TBSP BAKING POWDER

FOR THE CHANTILLY CREAM
100ML (3½ OZ) DOUBLE CREAM
2TBSP CASTER SUGAR
1 VANILLA POD

blood orange and champagne jelly with honey madeleines & chantilly cream

A very chic and pretty dessert. If you don't want to go to the bother of unmoulding the jellies, allow them to set in pretty glasses.

Remove the peel and pith from the oranges using a very sharp knife. Segment the oranges by cutting out the flesh between the membranes. Put the segments aside. Combine the champagne and sugar syrup and squeeze the juice from what is left of the oranges into the mixture.

Cover the gelatine with cold water and leave to soak. Heat 100ml (3½fl oz) of the orange syrup mixture just to hand-heat. Lift the gelatine out of the water, squeezing out the excess water, and add it to the warm orange syrup mixture. Dissolve the gelatine in this by stirring. Add the dissolved gelatine to the remaining orange syrup mixture and pass through a sieve. Place the orange segments in 4 ramekins or glasses, cover with the liquid and set in the fridge.

For the madeleines, preheat the oven to 190ºC/375ºF/gas mark 5. Beat the sugar, eggs and honey together until pale. In a pan, heat the butter until just turning brown and add the flour. Cook for 4–5 minutes over a gentle heat. Combine this with the egg mixture and the baking powder. Spoon the mixture into well buttered and floured madeleine tins and bake for 15 minutes, or until golden. Leave in the tins for a couple of minutes before carefully removing and leaving to cool on a wire rack.

For the chantilly cream whisk the cream with the sugar. Scrape the seeds out of the vanilla pod with a knife and add them to the cream.

If you are going to unmould the jellies, dip their containers briefly in hot water (this just loosens the jelly) and invert on to plates. Serve 2 madeleines with each turned-out portion of jelly and a spoonful of chantilly, or serve the jellies in glasses with the chantilly and the madeleines.

In winter, they light the fires at about 11am
and the crackle and smell of burning logs
and the gentle buzz of pre-lunch activity
makes it the perfect place just to hang out
with a coffee and the papers.'

All the pubs in this book are special, but this one has a particular claim on my heart. Not only is it near my home (not just around the corner, unfortunately), but it is also, to my mind, the perfect local.

The Carpenter's Arms is poised comfortably between homely and smart. Less bare and stripped down than most urban gastropubs, it has cushions on the wooden banquettes, lamps with woven shades that hang low over the tables and fairy lights twinkling in the little courtyard outside.

Chef Paul Adams is one of a growing breed of chefs, mostly in their early to mid-thirties, who have worked with Alastair Little for a significant amount of time and owe much to his style and ethos. These chefs want to turn out great food but do not want 'fine dining'. They like to work across all sections of the kitchen – making their own bread and ice-cream, if they fancy it – and have a penchant for being at the coalface rather than overseeing a team from on high.

Paul's food is unfussy and full of flavour and integrity. It is not particularly Mediterranean, despite Little's influence, but fairly robustly English (though he goes back time and time again to Larousse and a few Med do dishes turn up). There's a good mixture of cheap ingredients made into something grand and a few genuinely grand things. You will always find oysters on the menu plus plenty of wild mushrooms and lobster, in season, alongside such ingredients as ham hocks and lentils. At lunchtime, you might be lucky enough to find the hot salt-beef sandwich on the menu, served with beetroot relish and a small cup of hot soup. Their mutton broth is rich and sticky and will warm you to the core. Game is key and much is made of old-fashioned preserves – chicken liver parfait comes with pickled damsons and bread-and-butter pickles, for example.

Paul believes that a pub allows him to cook in a way that would not be possible in a restaurant. He has more freedom to do what he likes here and The Carpenter's is very much his baby. Owner Simon Cherry oversaw the design of the place but gives Paul a free hand when it comes to the cooking.

The staff come from all over the world – Sweden, Brazil, Turkey and America – and are mad keen on food. They are ably overseen by Paul's girlfriend Matilda Jaine, who is the daughter of Tom Jaine – one of the most distinguished food publishers in the country – and knows her wine. Quite a team. I only wish it were around the corner.

the carpenter's arms

91 BLACK LION LANE, LONDON, W6 9BG • TEL 020 8741 8386
SERVES LUNCH AND DINNER EVERY DAY

'Paul cooked for Alastair Little both at his
restaurant in Frith Street and at Lancaster Road
and it shows: his food is unfussy; full of flavour
and integrity; and does what it says on the tin.'

serves 4

4 X 500G (1LB) LIVE LOBSTERS

2 TBSP SEA SALT

2 TBSP CASTER SUGAR

400G (14OZ) SAMPHIRE

1KG (2LB 4OZ) JERSEY ROYAL POTATOES

FOR THE BASIL BUTTER

1 BUNCH OF BASIL

3 CLOVES GARLIC, ROUGHLY CHOPPED

JUICE OF 1 LEMON

150G (5½OZ) UNSALTED BUTTER, SOFTENED

baked lobster, jersey royals, samphire & basil butter

A luxurious treat. Serve with asparagus if you can't get samphire.

To make the basil butter, put the leaves into a food processor with the garlic, lemon juice and butter and whiz until blended. Put into the fridge until firm enough to handle. Form the butter into a sausage shape and wrap in greaseproof paper, twisting the ends to seal it firmly. Keep in the fridge until needed.

Bring a pan of water (large enough to fit 4 lobsters) to the boil. Add the salt and sugar. Half fill your sink with iced water. Take one lobster at a time, place on a chopping board and put the tip of a large knife on the lobster's head where there is a natural cross. With one firm tap push the knife into the lobster. Immediately plunge the lobsters into the boiling water for 15 seconds and then into the iced water for 10 minutes. Drain really well and chill.

Cut the lobsters in half lengthways. Remove all the innards (all the stuff that doesn't look like good meat) but leave the tail-meat intact. Wipe out each lobster to remove any gunk left behind in the shell. Remove the claws, take any meat from them and put it into the cleaned lobster shells, along with the tail meat.

Pick through the samphire and remove any twiggy stalks. Boil the potatoes until nearly cooked so they can be reheated and finished quickly. Preheat the oven to 220°C/425°F/gas mark 7 and put two pans on to boil. Put the lobsters into a roasting tin. Lightly smear the flesh of the lobster with the basil butter and season. Roast for 10 minutes. After 9 minutes, drop the samphire and Jersey royals into the pans of boiling water. Take out the lobsters and place on warm dishes. Drain the samphire and potatoes and add them to the roasting tin. Add some more basil butter to the tin and toss until it has melted all over the samphire and potatoes. On warm plates serve a portion of potatoes and samphire with a lobster laid accross the top.

serves 4

8 JERUSALEM ARTICHOKES
15G (½OZ) UNSALTED BUTTER
SPRIG OF THYME
SALT AND PEPPER
100G (3½OZ) CHANTERELLE MUSHROOMS
4TBSP CHOPPED FLAT-LEAF PARSLEY
1 SMOKED EEL, SKINNED AND FILLETED
1 HEAD OF CHICORY
¼ HEAD OF RADICCHIO
DUCK FAT OR OLIVE OIL
4 SLICES SOURDOUGH BREAD
SPLASH SHERRY VINEGAR
SALT AND PEPPER
3TBSP CHOPPED CHIVES

sauté of smoked eel, jerusalem artichoke & parsley

I've made this so many times since I first ate it. If you don't want to push the boat out to buy chanterelles then other interesting cultivated mushrooms, or even good field mushrooms (sliced) will do.

Peel the Jerusalem artichokes and cut into rounds. Slowly cook these in butter with the sprig of thyme, salt and pepper. Leave to cool.

Pick through the chanterelles, removing any dirt. Pull the leaves off the parsley. Cut the smoked eel into 2cm-long (about 1 inch) diamonds. Remove the hearts from the chicory and radicchio (discard these bits) and finely shred the leaves.

Warm a large frying pan and add 2 tbsp duck fat or olive oil. While this is heating up lightly toast the bread and spread one side with some duck fat or drizzle with olive oil then leave somewhere to keep warm. Increase the heat under the pan and carefully add the Jerusalem artichokes and the chanterelles. Cook for 20 seconds and season; throw in the smoked eel, chicory, radicchio and parsley. Toss until warm and lightly wilted, then add a good splash of sherry vinegar, toss a few more times, place on warm toast and sprinkle with the chives.

serves 6

6 COD FILLETS, ABOUT 200G (7OZ)
  EACH
2TBSP OLIVE OIL
SALT AND PEPPER
45G (1½OZ) BUTTER
1 LEMON

FOR THE BEANS
500G (1LB 2OZ) DRIED BUTTER BEANS
2 ONIONS
4 CELERY STICKS
2 CARROTS
2TBSP OLIVE OIL
6 MORCILLA SAUSAGES (SPANISH BLACK
  PUDDING), ABOUT 350G (12 OZ)
4 CLOVES OF GARLIC, FINELY CHOPPED
1½TSP SMOKED PAPRIKA

3 SPRIGS OF THYME
2 SPRIGS OF ROSEMARY
2 BAY LEAVES
2 X 400G (14OZ) CANS CHOPPED
  TOMATOES
2TBSP COARSELY CHOPPED
  FLAT-LEAF PARSLEY
SALT AND PEPPER

FOR THE AÏOLI
3 EGG YOLKS
4 CLOVES GARLIC
JUICE OF 1 LEMON
SALT AND PEPPER
150ML (¼ PINT) EXTRA VIRGIN
  OLIVE OIL

roast cod, butter beans, black pudding & aïoli

Some of the best things about Spanish cooking – beans, black pudding and garlic mayonnaise – are here in one dish. What more could you ask for?

Soak the beans for 8 hours then drain, place in a pan of fresh water and simmer for 1½ hours. The beans should be firm but cooked through. Lightly salt the fillets of cod, wrap loosely in clingfilm and put in the fridge. Cut the onions, celery and carrots into cubes about half the size of a butter bean. Heat the olive oil for the beans in a broad pan. Peel the skin from the morcilla and cut into thumbnail-sized pieces. Put the chopped vegetables, garlic and smoked paprika into the warming oil and sweat over a low heat until softening. Add the morcilla and herbs and cook for a further 6 minutes. Add the tomatoes, turn the heat up to full and cook for 5 minutes, stirring continuously. Turn the heat down to medium, drain the butter beans and add to the mixture. Cook for a further 15 minutes on a medium heat. Remove from the heat, put into a container and allow to rest overnight. To make the aïoli, blend the egg yolks, garlic and half the lemon juice in a food processor. Pour the oil into the blender in a steady stream until it forms a thick sauce. Taste and adjust the seasoning and lemon juice. Keep in the fridge until needed.

Preheat the oven to 220°C/425°F/gas mark 7. Heat an ovenproof, nonstick pan large enough to hold the 4 fillets of cod. Pour in a couple of tablespoons of olive oil, throw in some sea salt and add the cod. Put a knob of butter and a grinding of pepper onto each fillet. Place in the oven for 7 minutes, or until the fish is cooked through. Meanwhile, heat the butter bean mixture. Remove the cod from the oven and squeeze some lemon juice over it. Add chopped parsley to the beans and check the seasoning. Spoon the bean mixture on to warmed plates and place the cod on top, skin-side up. Finish with a spoonful of aïoli.

serves 8

2 HAM HOCKS, SMOKED OR
   UNSMOKED, WHICHEVER YOU PREFER
2 ONIONS, HALVED
1 SMALL HEAD OF CELERY, CHOPPED
   INTO LARGE PIECES
2 CARROTS
1 BAY LEAF
2 SPRIGS OF THYME
8 CLOVES
8 BLACK PEPPERCORNS
3 BLADES MACE
300G (10½OZ) CURLY PARSLEY
3 LEAVES GELATINE

2 LARGE SHALLOTS, DICED
6 GHERKINS, DICED
1TSP CAPERS, CHOPPED
1TBSP ENGLISH MUSTARD
SALAD LEAVES, SUCH AS WATERCRESS
   OR LAMB'S LETTUCE, TO SERVE

FOR THE NECTARINE SALAD
1½ CINNAMON STICKS
200G (7OZ) CASTER SUGAR
½TSP CRUMBLED DRIED CHILLI
1 STAR ANISE
175ML (6FL OZ) WHITE WINE VINEGAR
6 FIRM BUT RIPE NECTARINES

ham hock and parsley terrine with marinated nectarine & cinnamon salad

This is a fantastic salad. Even if you don't make the terrine, try the salad with cold cuts or roast duck breast.

Rinse the ham hocks and soak in water for 1 hour. Drain, place in a large pan and cover with water. Bring to the boil, drain and cover with fresh water. Bring to the boil again. Add the vegetables, herbs and spices. Place 2 heavy plates on the ham to keep it submerged and simmer for 2 hours. Take off the heat and put the ham hocks on to a tray to cool. Sieve the stock into a clean pan and reduce by a third, checking it hasn't become too salty. Add fresh water if need be.

Blanch the parsley in hot water until soft then plunge into cold water, drain and squeeze in a dry cloth. Chop finely. Soak the gelatine in cold water until soft. Shred the meat from the ham hocks, discarding a third of the fat. Place the remaining fat in a bowl and add the shallots, gherkins, capers and parsley along with the mustard, and mulch together so the fat breaks down. Add the ham and mix thoroughly. Check the seasoning. Line a large terrine mould or loaf tin with clingfilm. Warm 300ml (½ pint) of the ham stock (but don't boil). Drain the gelatine and add to the stock, whisking to help the gelatine dissolve. Put the ham mix into the lined terrine, pat down gently and then pour over the stock and gelatine mix. Chill overnight.

To make the salad, put all the dry ingredients into a pan along with the vinegar and simmer for 8 minutes. Cut the nectarine into eighths, removing the stones; place in a shallow dish and pour the cinnamon liquor on to them through a fine sieve. Cover with clingfilm and chill for 12 hours. Serve a slice of the terrine per person with warm bread, the nectarine segments and some salad leaves lightly dressed with the cinnamon liquor.

serves 10

1 SALTED BRISKET (IT WILL WEIGH ABOUT
  2.5KG/5LB 8OZ)
½ BUNCH FLAT-LEAF PARSLEY
1 ONION
1 HEAD CELERY
2 CARROTS
6 CLOVES
1 SPRIG OF THYME
1 BAY LEAF
SOURDOUGH, RYE OR CARAWAY BREAD, TO SERVE

hot salt-beef sandwich, beetroot relish & bread-and-butter pickles

You don't have to make both the relish and the pickles (*see* the recipes overleaf) but that's the way Paul serves it. He also presents it with a salad of grated carrot tossed with dressing and toasted caraway seeds. This is great for a Saturday lunch, with baked fruit or a pie for afters.

Soak the brisket in water for 3 hours, changing the water frequently. Rinse the beef then place in a pan with enough water to cover and bring to the boil. Drain, add fresh water and bring to the boil again. Into a clean pan put the parsley, onion, celery, carrots, cloves, thyme, bay leaf and the brisket. Cover with water and place 2 heavy plates on top of the brisket to keep it submerged. Simmer for 8 hours, keeping the water level topped up.

After 8 hours check that the meat is tender. If it isn't you should continue to cook it. Leave the beef to cool in the stock for 1 hour, then remove and place on a tray to allow to cool for a further 1½ hours. Tightly wrap the beef in clingfilm and chill. Reduce the cooking liquor by a third or until it is rich and brothy. Pass through a fine sieve and allow to cool, then chill.

To serve, heat up the salt-beef broth, take the clingfilm off the brisket and slice the meat. Add the beef slices to the broth and heat gently without boiling. In a warm oven, warm thick-cut slices of whatever bread you are using. Make sandwiches out of the warm beef and bread, using butter and mustard to your taste. Serve with beetroot relish, bread-and-butter pickles and a small bowl of the warm broth per person.

bread & butter pickles

10 BABY CUCUMBERS
SEA SALT
3 ONIONS
2TSP ONION SEEDS
½TSP CARAWAY SEEDS
1TSP CHILLI FLAKES
3TSP GROUND TURMERIC
600ML (1 PINT) WHITE WINE VINEGAR
175G (6OZ) CASTER SUGAR

Top and tail the baby cucumbers and peel the skin so that you end up with alternating stripes of skin and flesh. Cut into slices about 5mm (¼ inch) thick. Line a flat tray with a clean cloth and place the baby cucumbers onto it; sprinkle with 2tbsp sea salt. Cover the tray with clingfilm and chill for 6 hours in the fridge.

Remove the cucumbers from the fridge and tip onto a clean cloth. Bundle up and squeeze out the water with three turns of the cloth. Peel and halve the onions, remove and discard the roots and thinly slice the flesh.

In a large pan gently toast the onion seeds, caraway seeds and chilli flakes; add the turmeric, white wine vinegar and sugar. Stir, bring to the boil and then remove from the heat. In a non-metallic mixing bowl combine the onions and the cucumber. Pour over the warm vinegar mixture, stir, cover with clingfilm and chill.

beetroot relish

150ML (¼ PINT) RED WINE VINEGAR
100G (3½OZ) CASTER SUGAR
9 COOKED BEETROOT, PEELED AND GRATED
225G (8OZ) GRATED FRESH HORSERADISH

Mix the vinegar and sugar in a heavy-based pan and bring to boil.

Add the beetroot and horseradish and cook slowly on a moderate heat until a spoon pulled through the mixture leaves an empty channel. Cool and chill.

serves 6

100G (3½OZ) CASTER SUGAR
300ML (10FL OZ) WATER
400ML (14FL OZ) PIMMS
JUICE OF 1 LEMON

FOR THE FRUIT SALAD

300G (10½OZ) GRANULATED SUGAR
400ML (12FL OZ) WATER
15 UNSPRAYED PELARGONIAM LEAVES
1 ORANGE, PEELED AND SEGMENTED
8 STRAWBERRIES, HULLED AND HALVED
SEEDS AND PULP FROM
   4 PASSION FRUITS

1 MANGO, PEELED AND FLESH CUT
   FROM THE STONE
½ SMALL CHARENTAIS MELON, CUT
   INTO SLICES AND SKIN REMOVED
2 KIWI FRUIT, PEELED
1 APPLE, HALVED AND CORED
2 PLUM TOMATOES, PEELED
   AND DESEEDED
½ CUCUMBER, PEELED AND DESEEDED
1 CARROT
SMALL BUNCH OF MINT
SMALL BUNCH OF BASIL

pelargoniam-scented fruit salad & pimms granita

Paul makes this with scented geranium leaves, which smell a bit like roses
and wild strawberries. You can get the plants in nurseries but if this proves
impossible, use a dash of rose water or just do without. The mint and basil
add a lovely perfume anyway.

To make the granita, put the sugar and water in a pan, stirring well to dissolve the sugar. Leave
to cool and add all the other ingredients. Pour into a broad, shallow container and freeze for
24 hours. Fork the mixture up after 2 hours and return to the freezer, forking it a few more times
during the freezing process – you want the result to be fluffy ice.

For the fruit salad, put the sugar and water in a pan and heat slowly, stirring to help the sugar
dissolve. Bring to the boil and leave for 4 minutes. Add the pelargoniam leaves and reduce the
syrup by an eighth by boiling again. Leave to cool.

To make the salad, cube the fruit, tomato, cucumber and carrot into 1.5cm (¾ inch) pieces. Shred
the mint and basil finely and, just before serving, toss through the salad with the pelargonium
syrup. Serve the fruit in glasses, with a healthy spoonful of the granita.

the best of the rest

the anchor and hope

Owned by Mike Belben, who, together with David Eyre, started the whole gastropub revolution when they opened The Eagle in Farringdon Road, this place saw him taking gastropub dining onto a whole new level. I don't know a soul who doesn't love The Anchor and Hope. It's quite a sprawling place in Waterloo, with no apparent charms on the outside, but once inside it has the buzz of an eaterie in Barcelona. It's loud, it's exuberant, it's thronged and the food is realer than real – Lancashire hotpot, pot-roast pork with gooseberries, steak and kidney pie, buttermilk pudding with rhubarb. Robust, gutsy, elemental – you run out of words muscular enough to describe the cooking. Drinkers come here too – this is a proper pub and not just a dining destination. It's annoyingly democratic – you can't reserve. Just pitch up. And you need to get there early, believe me.

36 The Cut, Waterloo, London, SE1 8LP, Tel. 020 7928 9898 Serves lunch (except Monday) and dinner (except Sunday).

the brown dog

A really sweet place tucked away among the cottagey bit of Barnes, the epitome of well-heeled, leafy suburbia known as Little Chelsea, The Brown Dog has really established itself among the young professionals who live nearby. The décor may seem to be a mish-mash – copper-coloured globe lights alongside wrought iron sconces, sturdy old tables and chairs, eclectic prints – but it works really well and feels evolved rather than designed. On the menu you might find potted shrimps, braised oxtail with horseradish mash and hispi cabbage and roast bone marrow on toast with parsley salad. It's strong on English classics but there are plenty of nods to France as well, such as rillettes and onion soup. A great little neighbourhood local.

28 Cross Street, Barnes, London, SW13 0AP Tel. 020 8392 2200, www.thebrowndog.co.uk Serves lunch and dinner every day.

the duke of sussex

Chiswick was pretty well-off for good dining pubs anyway, and then along came The Duke of Sussex, a handsome, bright place right on a street corner. It's a class act, kitted out in glossy gastropub style – chandeliers, leather banquettes, high ceilings – and the food, from Chris Payne (who used to cook at the estimable St John's in Archway), is excellent. The menu steers away from gastropub classics and instead features international food: salt-cod croquettes, Brazilian pork and bean stew, brawn with gherkins, honeycomb ice-cream – the chef never settles on just one country.

75 South Parade, London, W4 5LF, Tel. 020 8742 8801 Serves lunch and dinner every day.

the gun

It isn't the easiest place to find, tucked away as it is in a little residential area amidst all the urban gloss of Docklands, but it's worth the trek. This is one of duo Tom and Ed Martin's successful gastropub empire and, in my opinion, the best. There's a lovely bar with linen-covered tables, a very popular outdoor area, and a smart dining room upstairs. Naval paraphernalia is prominent throughout but it's all in the best possible taste. Food is sensible stuff for a pub and extremely well turned out (though the quality is variable – you get good and bad days here). Pints of prawns with mayo, fish pie and gooseberry crumble are just what you want. Despite being full of city workers – who come and go in a steady stream – it's very laidback. I'm surprised any of them return to their offices.

27 Coldharbour, Docklands, London E14 9NS Tel. 020 7515 5222, www.thegundocklands.com Serves lunch and dinner every day.

the horseshoe

This is a big buzzy bar, very youthful, very laid back, with its own micro-brewery in the basement, frequented by as many drinkers as diners. It's an open, modern space (so don't come looking for snugs or cosy corners) though there is a quieter and more intimate dining area at the back of the place on a raised level. The food is contemporary, interesting and ungimmicky. And they care about sourcing. 'Quality produce from farm to fork', trumpets the menu. There are some truly original dishes such as a salad of watermelon and ham hock, which you imagine won't work but does, and the Bresse chicken for two keeps the punters coming back.

28 Heath Street, Hampstead, London, NW3 6TE Tel. 020 7431 7206. Serves lunch and dinner every day.

the marquess tavern

A bit of contemporary country in an Islington backwater, the Marquess has many adoring fans so book, especially if you're planning to have Sunday lunch here (it is famed for its Sunday lunches). Enter and you are lulled by buttermilk-coloured walls, enamel jugs, flowers, mirrors, big roomy leather sofas and country furniture. That's not to say the space isn't elegant – it is – but it doesn't feel at all like an urban pub. And the cooking has a rural flavour, too. It's the best of British here so expect potted salmon with pickled cucumber, old-fashioned pies, crab mayonnaise and duck with carrots and potatoes. Interesting English bottles on the wine list and British cheeses too.

32 Canonbury Street, Islington, London, N1 2TB
Tel. 020 7354 2975, www.marquesstavern.co.uk/index.asp
Serves lunch and dinner every day.

the norfolk arms

It was the tapas that drew me here – they have a huge range – but it's the rest of the food that keeps me coming back. The Norfolk Arms occupies a good big, bright space in Bloomsbury. It's an old pub but the interior is kept light by the use of bleached wooden tables and chairs, and chicly washed out tea-towels as tablemats, though there's nothing designed about the place. Just a nice eclectic collection of worn furniture. The cooking is not of the kind that will make you gasp – it's simple and doesn't show off – but it's very well done and just the kind of food you want a city pub to be offering. Lots of it has a Spanish flavour – pork belly with chorizo and lentils, squid and octopus salad, fish with black pudding, and there's a good selection of sherries. Bloomsbury is not the easiest place to find pleasurable sustenance – endless charmless sandwich shops – so this is a good spot to know about.

28 Leigh Street, London, WC1H 9EP
Tel. 020 7388 3937, www.norfolkarms.co.uk
Serves lunch every day and dinner (except Sunday).

the only running footman

Barnaby Meredith, the owner here, is to be much admired for his additions to the London pub scene. I love The House in Islington (seriously good shepherd's pie) and he has The Bull in Highgate as well. This, a small pub in Mayfair with a smart dining room upstairs, is his latest venture and the emphasis is very much on British food. You get fish pie, pork pie and a changing 'pie of the day' as well as lasagne (I know, it makes your heart sink but it's a very good one, and is something of a Brit pub classic), Eton mess and steamed chocolate pudding. The pub opens at 7:30am for breakfast (when you can order a wonderful omelette 'Arnold Bennett'), which is a great idea and excellent value. A good pub to know about in an area not famed for less expensive places to dine. A winner.

5 Charles Street, London, W1J 5DE
Tel. 020 7499 2988, www.themeredithgroup.co.uk
Serves lunch and dinner every day.

the rosendale

A big, high ceilinged Victorian pile in leafy West Dulwich with huge windows, this is a swanky number. Brown leather banquettes and candy-striped fabric in the dining area make you feel as though you are sitting in an expensive chocolate box, though the bar area is slightly less chic. This is not your bare boards and rickety tables gastroboozer, though. There are separate menus and the dining room fare comes with more daubs and drizzles. I'd go for the bar food – Landes chicken with mushrooms, steak sandwich, braised ox cheeks with mash. Desserts are the weakest link. The great wine list, with some 30 by the glass, is perhaps its biggest draw, and why I return. It's no surprise to find that the owner was a sommelier in some of London's swankier eateries. The service is remarkably good and well informed.

65 Rosendale Road, London, SE21 8EZ, Tel. 020 8670 0812
www.therosendale.co.uk. Serves lunch and dinner every day.

the thomas cubitt

For sheer elegance this is one of the loveliest pubs in London. Wood panelling, eclectic prints, Georgian proportions; it is drop dead gorgeous. As well as the big sprawling downstairs bar, there's a swish dining room upstairs with a separate and swankier menu. Food in the bar encompasses brasserie dishes – chicken Caesar salad, squid with caper and anchovy mayo, fish and chips – though you can also enjoy good old-fashioned English pies. Elizabeth Street is a great foodie haunt, too. Both Poilane bakery and Baker and Spice are here. So you can turn up for breakfast in Elizabeth Street and, well, never leave…

44 Elizabeth Street, Belgravia, London, SW1W 9PA
Tel. 020 7730 6060, www.thethomascubitt.co.uk
Serves lunch and dinner every day.

the southeast

Two months after I'd eaten at The Granville, I was still thinking about the food: a small white bowl of vegetable risotto (carrots, peas, broad beans); a pink piece of lamb rump served with its cooking juices; burnt cream with rhubarb sorbet. There was also a warm duvet of salt-crusted focaccia and a little plate of homemade fudge and chocolate truffles, which came with a perfect espresso.

Good – but nothing remarkable, you might think. But every dish had pure, clean flavours. The lamb was a prime bit of meat and the chef had got the best out of it. The risotto was one of the loveliest I'd ever tasted – and no wonder, since the vegetables had been picked from the pub's garden only a few hours before. I'd just come back from a two-week holiday in France and hadn't eaten anything nearly as good. This place serves up a grand meal in simple style.

The Granville is sister to another dining pub, The Sportsman in Seasalter, owned by self-taught chef Stephen Harris. Stephen's sister Gabrielle runs The Granville, whose partner is the chef, Jim Shave, formerly a chef at The Sportsman. Jim, like Stephen, has a holistic approach to cooking and a big thing about 'terroir': he believes that the flavour of a dish comes directly from the environment in which its ingredients were produced. He sources what he can from the people around him and uses every bit of the animals he buys. The two chefs do as much as they can themselves: curing meat, smoking foods, baking bread. Stephen even makes his own salt from seawater. They do all this for reasons of taste and quite simply because they enjoy getting as close as possible to the food they are producing.

'We had great cod on the menu last night,' says Jim. 'We went fishing yesterday afternoon after lunchtime service and caught enough fish for dinner. It was on with spinach and potatoes and horseradish butter – all from the garden, even the horseradish. And Stephen churned the butter. We didn't make the white wine that went into the fish but not bad, huh?'

Jim is an instinctive cook and isn't looking to do anything radical, just to intensify flavours. He works in the pub's garden every afternoon (he and Stephen want this to expand enough to support both pubs and supply locals who want to be part of a box scheme) and Stephen, in turn, will do smoking and curing for The Sportsman.

Lucky are the diners who live near enough to eat the fruits of this kind of passion. The Granville is a place where the terms 'home-grown' and 'hand-made' can be properly applied. And you can taste it in every forkful.

the granville

STREET END, LOWER HARDRES, KENT, CT4 7AL • TEL 01227 700402
SERVES LUNCH (EXCEPT MONDAY) AND DINNER (EXCEPT SUNDAY)

serves 6

FOR THE BALSAMIC VINEGAR
DRESSING
3 TBSP BALSAMIC VINEGAR
12 TBSP EXTRA VIRGIN OLIVE OIL
OLIVE OIL
BUTTER
6 SPRIGS OF THYME
6 CLOVES GARLIC, CRUSHED
12 LARGE FIELD MUSHROOMS OR
   SMALL HORSE MUSHROOMS,
   CLEANED
6 THICK SLICES GOOD COARSE
   COUNTRY BREAD
SALT AND PEPPER

FOR THE TAPENADE
500G (1LB 2OZ) BLACK KALAMATA
   OLIVES, PITTED
75G (2 ½OZ) SALTED ANCHOVIES
75G (2 ½OZ) CAPERS
SMALL BUNCH OF FLAT-LEAF PARSLEY
SMALL BUNCH OF BASIL
2 CLOVES GARLIC
75ML (2 ½FL OZ) RED WINE
50ML (2FL OZ) EXTRA VIRGIN
   OLIVE OIL

TO SERVE
SORREL, CRESS, CHERVIL AND OTHER
   WILD LEAVES (CHICKWEED AND WATER
   CELERY, FOR EXAMPLE)

garlic & thyme roasted mushrooms on tapenade toast

This makes a good lunch or snack dish.

Put all the tapenade ingredients in a food processor and blitz until completely smooth.

For the dressing, whisk the balsamic vinegar and olive oil in a bowl.

Preheat the oven to 200°C/400°F/gas mark 6. Put a good glug of olive oil and a good knob of butter into an ovenproof frying pan. Add the thyme and garlic and allow the butter to foam. Place the mushrooms in the pan stalk-side-down and fry for about 2 minutes or until they are golden brown. Turn over and place the pan in the oven for 2 minutes. Toast the bread and spread with a good layer of tapenade then place in the oven to warm the tapenade. When the mushrooms are cooked, season them with salt and pepper.

To serve, place the slices of tapenade toast on plates then put 2 mushrooms on each slice. Mix the leaves in a bowl with the balsamic dressing. Place next to the toast and spoon the mushroom roasting juices around the plate.

serves 6

6 x 175G (6OZ) TURBOT FILLETS, SKINNED
150G (5½OZ) UNSALTED BUTTER
SEA SALT
125ML (4FL OZ) WHITE WINE
SMALL BUNCH OF FLAT-LEAF PARSLEY, CHOPPED
JUICE OF ½ LEMON

FOR THE TARTARE SAUCE
100G (3½OZ) CHOPPED GHERKINS
100G (3½OZ) SHALLOTS, DICED
SMALL BUNCH OF CHIVES, CHOPPED
100G (3½OZ) CAPERS, RINSED OF SALT, BRINE
  OR VINEGAR
350G (12OZ) GOOD BOUGHT MAYONNAISE

turbot with tartare sauce

They get fantastic turbot at The Granville so believe in treating it simply.
This is great served with spring greens or wilted spinach.

Preheat the grill to medium. Place the turbot fillets in a shallow roasting tin big enough to take all the fillets comfortably. Take one-third of the butter and divide into 6 slices. Place 1 slice of butter on each of the fillets. Season the fish with salt and pour the wine into the tin.

Place a square of damp, nonstick baking paper over the fish, ensuring all the fillets are covered – this helps to protect the fish from the heat. Place the tin under the preheated grill to cook gently for 10 minutes or until the fish is cooked through.

Make the tartare sauce by mixing the gherkins, shallots, chives and capers with the mayonnaise.

When the fish has cooked, place the fillets on warm plates (put the fish on top of the wilted spinach, if using). Keep warm in a low oven.

Sieve the fish cooking juices into a saucepan and place on a high heat to reduce by half. Add the chopped parsley and stir in. Add the remaining butter and whisk in. Season with lemon juice and salt.

Pour the sauce over the fish and place a spoonful of tartare sauce on top of each fillet. Serve immediately.

lunchtime service and caught enough fish for dinner! It was on with spinach and potatoes and horseradish butter – all from the garden, even the horseradish. And Stephen churned the butter. We didn't make the white wine that went into the fish but not bad, huh?"

serves 6

FOR THE CEP STOCK

250G (9OZ) DRIED CEPS

1 CARROT, SLICED

1 ONION, SLICED

1 CELERY STICK, SLICED

4 CLOVES GARLIC, CRUSHED

3 SPRIGS OF THYME

3 SPRIGS OF ROSEMARY

5 BLACK PEPPERCORNS

1 LITRE (1¾ PINTS) WATER

FOR THE CEP SAUCE

1 LITRE (1¾ PINTS) GOOD
 HOMEMADE CHICKEN STOCK

600ML (1 PINT) DOUBLE CREAM

A FEW DROPS TRUFFLE OIL

SALT

LEMON JUICE, TO TASTE

15G (½OZ) COLD UNSALTED BUTTER

LEAVES FROM 3 SPRIGS OF TARRAGON,
 CHOPPED

3TBSP VEGETABLE OIL, SUCH AS
 PEANUT OR SUNFLOWER

25G (1OZ) UNSALTED BUTTER

6 FREE-RANGE CHICKEN BREASTS
 (225G/8OZ) EACH)

roast chicken breast with cep sauce

You can also serve this earthy, musky sauce with a whole roast chicken.

To make the cep sauce first make the stock. Put all the ingredients in a large saucepan, bring to the boil and simmer for 20 minutes. Pass through a sieve. Put the cep stock and the chicken stock into a saucepan and reduce by rapidly boiling until you have a thick, dark liquid. Add the cream and bring to the boil, then simmer until the sauce coats the back of a spoon. Add a few drops of truffle oil, and then salt and lemon juice to taste.

To cook the chicken breasts, preheat the oven to 110°C/225°F/gas mark ¼. Heat the oil in a frying pan and add the butter. Brown the skin of the breast then transfer to the oven. Keep basting until the core temperature of the chicken reaches 65°C. If you don't have a meat thermometer this should take about 30 minutes. Check the chicken is cooked – there should be no trace of pinkness. Remove from the oven, cover and rest for 5 minutes.

Heat the cep sauce and add a knob of butter and the chopped tarragon.

Serve the chicken with creamed cabbage and roast potatoes, and with the sauce spooned over the meat.

serves 6

FOR THE SORBET

1KG (2LB 4OZ) RHUBARB

350G (12OZ) GRANULATED SUGAR

JUICE OF ½ LEMON

A LITTLE SPACE DUST FOR SPRINKLING ON
  EACH SERVING (OPTIONAL)

FOR THE BURNT CREAM

425ML (¾ PINT) DOUBLE CREAM

1 VANILLA POD

5 EGG YOLKS

60G (2¼ OZ) GRANULATED SUGAR

CASTER SUGAR

rhubarb sorbet with burnt cream

The Sportsman, The Granville's sister pub, became famous for this dish.
The flavours are incredibly intense and contrast brilliantly. You don't have
to include the space dust but it adds to the taste experience.

Roughly chop the rhubarb and mix with the sugar. Leave for 24 hours.

Put the fruit and sugar in a blender and pulse to break up the rhubarb. Sieve so that you collect
the juice in a bowl, pressing down with the back of a spoon to extract as much as possible, then
leave the juice to settle in the fridge for 2 hours.

Skim the residue from the surface of the rhubarb juice, add the lemon juice then churn the bright
pink liquid in an ice-cream machine. If you don't have a machine, put in shallow containers and
freeze for 1–2 hours. Fork the sorbet into granules and return to the freezer. Repeat three or four
times. Put into shot glasses and keep in the freezer.

To make the burnt cream, bring the cream and vanilla pod to the boil. Meanwhile whisk the
egg yolks and sugar in a pan set over simmering water until the mixture thickens. Strain the hot
cream over the eggs and whisk until thick. Pass through a sieve into espresso cups and chill for
at least 2 hours. Sprinkle the surface of the creams thickly and evenly with caster sugar and
caramelize, either under a hot grill or with a blowtorch.

Sprinkle each rhubarb sorbet with a little space dust, if using, and serve the burnt cream alongside.

the best of the rest

carnarvon arms

The locals were worried about this one. Taken over and considerably spruced up (pale natural colours, bare boards, cool sofas), there was much anxiety that the Carnarvon would just become a restaurant or, at worst, a gastropub without soul. But the bar remains traditional, if clean-lined, and there are still ales on tap. Pubby dishes such as beef and ale pie are offered alongside more complex dishes such as pasta with crab and lobster or beef with Madeira. Smart bedrooms too.

Winchester Road, Whitway, Burghclere, Newbury, Hampshire, RG20 9LE
Tel. 01635 278222, www.carnarvonarms.com
Serves lunch and dinner every day, rooms available.

the peat spade

A darling, storybook place, this slightly reminds me of the cottage where Hansel and Gretel met their demise: red brick, cute, with windows made up of tiny panes. It was bought in 2005 by Andrew Clarke and Lucy Townsend and they've created beautiful bedrooms as well as a top-notch dining pub. Andrew is a former head chef of the Hotel du Vin in Winchester and his food is as pub food should be – hearty with a touch of refinement, and very well executed. There could be game terrine, braised faggots, Lancashire hotpot with pickled red cabbage or a sticky walnut and date pudding on the menu. A smart, relaxing, eminently tasteful bolthole.

Village Street, Longstock, Stockbridge, Hampshire, SO20 6DR, Tel. 01264 810612, www.peatspadeinn.co.uk
Serves lunch every day and dinner (except Sunday), rooms available.

the dining room at the railway hotel

A fabulously romantic place. If I was to be whisked away for an evening of tenderness and good dining, this is where I would want to go. And it's right opposite Faversham Station which lends it an extra bitter-sweet poignancy. There is both a dining room and a bar (though you can't eat in the bar). The bar is a bold space, with deep red walls and glowing furniture. The dining room is hung with oval mirrors and filled with old pale wooden tables. It's a girl dressed for Sunday school – pretty, sweet and old-fashioned. And the food conjures up as much romance as the setting: local cherry blossom pannacotta with griottine cherry syrup, Jerusalem artichoke soup with shavings of smoked duck, mackerel with horseradish and foraged leaves. This is real food, intelligently thought out and cooked with great skill.

Preston Street, Faversham, Kent, ME13 8PE
Tel. 01795 533173, www.railwayhotelfaversham.co.uk
Serves lunch (except Monday and Tuesday) and dinner (except Sunday, Monday and Tuesday), rooms available.

the fitzwalter arms

Steve Harris, chef-owner of the wonderful Michelin-starred Sportsman pub in Seasalter, tipped me off about this place. The chef here put in his time in Steve's kitchen and, judging from the food he is turning out, he had a great teacher. There's not a huge choice but the offerings are intelligent and what Steve calls 'the real deal'. Nothing is fancy, modish or presented just for effect. You can feast on pigeon breast with Puy lentils, super-slow-roasted pork belly with rhubarb compote and roast chicken with bread sauce. The décor hasn't been touched by the hands of designers or refurbishers – it's just a bog standard old-fashioned pub – but, as Steve says, at the Fitzwalter they like to keep it real.

The Street, Goodnestone, Kent, CT3 1PJ, Tel. 01304 840303
Serves lunch (every day) and dinner (except Sunday).

the albert arms

A gorgeous white-painted pub right on a street corner, money has been lavished on this pub. Despite the plain but handsome exterior, do not expect anything traditional. This place is modern, classy and sexy with smart tables and red leather chairs, but there are also eight ales from local micro-breweries (more than in most pubs) as well as 30 wines by the glass. The menu takes you back in time – in a good way! – as it touts old favourites such as prawn cocktail, grilled T-bone or sirloin steaks (the pub uses 28-day matured Angus beef) and chocolate profiteroles.

82 High Street, Esher, Surrey, KT10 9QS
Tel. 01372 465290, www.albertarms.com
Serves lunch every day and dinner (except Sunday), rooms available.

the parrot inn

Come here for lunch and you can pick up food for your dinner as there's a little shop smack in the middle of the pub with produce from the owners' farm and local fruit and veg growers. Charles and Linda Gotto used to own dining pubs in London but moved to Surrey in 2005. The food here comes from all corners of the globe and the menu is long. Choose from pork belly with chorizo, harissa-marinated lamb with couscous and terrines with homemade chutneys. The interior is a particularly lovely mishmash – rustic pale wood tables, church chairs, odd bits of furniture and sparkling glassware.

Forest Green, Dorking, Surrey, RH5 5RZ
Tel. 01306 621339, www.theparrot.co.uk
Serves lunch every day and dinner (except Sunday).

the swan inn

The Swan is modern, swish, cool, with chunky furniture and contemporary fabrics (it's a seriously classy interior), but still has the vestiges of a pub with a good range of ales at the bar (as well as a decent wine list) and some pre-gastropub classics on the menu, such as ham, egg and chips. There are also more modish offerings such as carpaccio, duck confit with red wine sauce, beef with onions and Madeira or salmon fish cakes with crème fraîche dressing. The Kelly Hoppen-inspired bedrooms are to die for.

Petworth Road, Chiddingfold, Guildford, Surrey, GU8 4TY
Tel. 01428 682073, www.theswaninn.biz
Serves lunch and dinner every day, rooms available.

the coach and horses

A much-loved local, this buzzy place is both cosy and elegant. Old wood-panelling and fires make it the perfect place to snuggle down in the winter and in the summer you can sit outside in the raised garden underneath the pub's huge maple tree. Fish from Seaford and lamb bred right by the pub are a highlight of the menu and practically all the food used comes from surrounding villages. Expect roast loin of pork with squash and rosemary, ham hock terrine with piccalilli and potato and thyme soup.

School Lane, Danehill, East Sussex, RH17 7JF
Tel. 01825 740369, www.coachandhorses.danehill.biz
Serves lunch every day and dinner (except Sunday).

the ginger pig

Behind the doors of what looks like an old boozer not far from the seafront, The Ginger Pig, one in a handful of eateries owned and run by Ben and Pamela McKellar, is every inch a classy, modern gastropub. Leather tub chairs and banquettes, taupe walls, a huge mirrored bar and burnt orange lampshades, everything is swish (maybe a little too much so – it could do with feeling a bit more lived in) and the food is local and gutsy-chic. Expect potted salt beef with beetroot and horseradish remoulade, veal cheeks braised in local ale and pork belly with creamed leeks.

3 Hove Street, Hove, Brighton and Hove, East Sussex, BN3 2TR, Tel. 01273 736123, www.gingermanrestaurants.com
Serves lunch and dinner every day.

the keepers arms

Good to see chef Matt Appleton at the helm here (I marked him as one to watch in my previous book on dining pubs) and he is still doing sterling work. His food is French – but not too complicated – and very confident and accomplished. Terrine of confit duck and foie gras, herb-crusted cod with a chive veloute and cumin-roasted South Downs lamb are all worth a detour. Aside from the food there's a warm welcome and an updated – though not too unpubby – interior. Big sofas that you can get lost in, beamed ceilings and oak floors will leave you wanting to linger.

Trotton, Petersfield, West Sussex, GU31 5ER
Tel. 01730 813724, www.keepersarms.co.uk
Serves lunch every day and dinner (except Sunday).

the royal oak inn

One of four classy pubs owned by Nick and Lisa Sutherland (see the others at the website below), this place combines rusticity with a contemporary feel. You're surrounded by bare bricks and stripped floors but there's a bright conservatory and outdoor heaters will warm you on cooler summer nights. Food is good, though the atmosphere and the lovely bedrooms are the bigger draw. The menu offers a whole panoply of modern standards – decent beefburgers, mushroom risotto and fish with coconut sauce.

Pook Lane, East Lavant, Chichester, West Sussex, PO18 0AX
Tel. 01243 527434, www.thesussexpub.co.uk
Serves lunch and dinner every day, rooms available.

heart of england

You might expect Emily Watkins, the chef and co-owner of The Kingham Plough, to be a ballet dancer. Doe-eyed and graceful, her hair pinned into a loose bun, wisps of which keep falling into her face, she looks as though pirouetting might suit her better than banging pots and pans. As with a dancer, her appearance belies a steely determination. She has always loved food but took an office job after university and lasted two months. She left a note for her mother saying she was off to Florence and, with no Italian, blagged her way into a restaurant job.

With no formal training, she felt the best place to go to next was somewhere she could really study the science of food. She wrote to Heston Blumenthal and after a day's trial landed a job at The Fat Duck. In 18 months she had become Heston's number two.

Eating the food at the Plough, you don't spot the Blumenthal influence immediately. The menu is full of simple modern fare, not odd pairings and innovative 'taste experiences'. There's a fine piece of brill with potato purée and fennel (a gorgeous study in beige; Emily doesn't feel the need to add colour to brighten dishes), loin of pork with lentils and wild mushrooms, potato gnocchi with squash and goat's cheese, and apple and butterscotch trifle. A lot of research is done into old local dishes. But she also applies science. I'm rather surprised when my loin of pork turns up looking as pink as bacon and send it back to the kitchen. Emily sears off the outside but explains that it is completely cooked. It's certainly the best bit of pork I have ever tasted. Her steaks, which are becoming famous, are cooked 'sous-vide', poached in vacuum-sealed bags until they are uniformly medium rare and then seared on the outside. She says: 'I am very interested in making food taste as much of itself as possible, in intensifying flavour. I don't want meat just to taste of caramelization and burnt butter, but to taste of meat.'

It goes without saying that her sourcing is impeccable and local. When Emily tells me what she gets from within a 5-mile radius I want to move to the village.

Emily, with unchef-like modesty, is slightly bewildered by the success of the Plough. Isn't a pub just a bit humble for someone of her culinary skills and background? 'This is what modern British pubs are now,' she says. 'We have managed to reinvent them. First there were manky old pubs, then gastropubs (which might have turned out reasonable Thai fishcakes). Now we have pubs with good ales, wines, local produce and modern British food. And this is the kind of place I want to cook in. When I come out of the kitchen at 11 at night and hear the place full of laughter and people having a great time, this is where I want to be. I just love it.'

the kingham plough

THE GREEN, KINGHAM, OXFORDSHIRE, OX7 6YD • TEL 01608 658327 • www.thekinghamplough.co.uk
SERVES LUNCH AND DINNER (EXCEPT SUNDAY DINNER), ROOMS AVAILABLE

serves 4

500G (1LB 2OZ) WATERCRESS, WASHED AND
  STEMS REMOVED
SPLASH OF WHITE WINE VINEGAR
5 DUCK EGGS (1 PER PERSON, PLUS 1 EXTRA
  FOR BREADCRUMBING)
PLAIN FLOUR
300G (10½OZ) FRESH BREADCRUMBS
VEGETABLE OIL, FOR DEEP-FRYING
150G (5½OZ) UNSMOKED BACON LARDONS

crisp duck egg with watercress sauce & bacon

This looks very impressive – the colours are wonderful – and it's actually very do-able at home.

To make the watercress sauce, bring a pan of water to the boil and have a bowl of iced water ready. Blanch the watercress in the boiling water for about 2 minutes until tender but still vibrant and green. Drain and plunge into the iced water. Lift out of the water and whizz in a blender with a little of the cold water until you have a smooth sauce.

For the eggs, bring a pan of water to a simmer and add a splash of white wine vinegar. Stir the water around to make a mini whirlpool and crack 4 of the eggs into the pan. Poach the eggs until the albumen is firm and the yolk soft (about 2 minutes: duck eggs cook more quickly than hen eggs). Lift out and place into iced water to chill. Then set them on kitchen paper to dry.

Beat the remaining egg. To breadcrumb the eggs, carefully place them one at a time in the flour, then dip in the beaten egg and lastly in the breadcrumbs.

Heat some vegetable oil in a saucepan to 180°C/350°F. Meanwhile, cook the bacon in a frying pan (there's no need to use any extra fat – the bacon will cook in the fat running out of it) until crisp, and warm through the sauce.

Gently lower the eggs into the hot oil and cook until crisp and golden. Lift out the eggs and place on to kitchen paper to absorb the excess oil. Place a spoonful of the sauce on to a plate, put some bacon on top and lastly a crisp egg.

serves 4

2 GRESSINGHAM DUCKS, OR OTHER GOOD
  QUALITY DUCKS
SALT AND PEPPER
ABOUT 800G (1LB 12OZ) GOOSE FAT
LEAVES FROM SMALL BUNCH OF SAGE
4 BANANA SHALLOTS
2 CARROTS
50G (2OZ) BUTTER
150G (5½OZ) GREEN LENTILS, WASHED
ABOUT 1 LITRE (1¾ PINTS) CHICKEN STOCK
2 HEADS OF CHICORY
SUGAR AND SALT

gressingham duck with evesham lentils & braised chicory

Duck, lentils and chicory go brilliantly together. You get earthiness, sweetness and bitterness all playing off each other.

Preheat the oven to 120°C/240°F/gas mark ½. Cut the breasts and legs (with the thighs) off the duck carcasses. Trim the breasts, scoring the skin. Season all the duck pieces and set the breasts aside. Melt the fat in a casserole dish, add the sage and put in the duck legs so they are covered in the fat. Cover with nonstick baking paper and cook in the oven for 3 hours, or until tender.

While the legs are cooking, prepare the lentils. Finely dice the shallot and carrot and sweat in half the butter until soft. Add the lentils and season. Cover with some of the stock, bring up to the boil and immediately turn down to a simmer. Cook until the lentils are tender but not falling apart (about 15 minutes). Slice the chicory in half lengthways and sprinkle liberally with sugar. Melt the rest of the butter in a frying pan and place the chicory, cut-and-sugared-side down, in the butter. Cook gently until golden and caramelized, then cover with the rest of the stock and gently simmer until tender. This can be done earlier and reheated when required.

Preheat the oven to 180°C/350°F/gas mark 4. To finish the dish, heat a heavy-based frying pan and place the duck breasts in it, skin-side down. There is no need to use any oil as there is plenty of fat in the skin. When the skin is golden and crispy, place in the oven for 8 minutes. It should be perfectly pink in the middle when you take it out. Cover, insulate and allow to rest for at least 10 minutes so that the juices can set. While the duck is resting put the rest of the dish together. Remove the legs from the goose fat, and crisp the skin in a hot frying pan. Warm through the lentils and chicory. Place a spoonful of lentils on each plate with a duck breast on top and half a caramelized chicory and a duck leg alongside.

'This is the kind of place I want to cook in. When I come out of the kitchen at 11 at night and hear the place full of laughter and people having a great time, this is where I want to be. I just love it.'

serves 4

3 BULBS OF FENNEL

1TSBP OLIVE OIL

50G (2OZ) BUTTER

SALT AND PEPPER

150G (5½) CHANTERELLE MUSHROOMS (OR ST GEORGE'S MUSHROOMS IN SPRING, OR PORTOBELLO OR OTHER GOOD QUALITY CULTIVATED MUSHROOMS)

LEAVES FROM 4 SPRIGS OF THYME, CHOPPED

3 EGGS

500ML (18FL OZ) DOUBLE CREAM

150G (5½OZ) SINGLE GLOUCESTER CHEESE (OR A MILD CHEDDAR), GRATED

1TBSP CHOPPED FLAT-LEAF PARSLEY

fennel & chanterelle bake

A simple, very satisfying dish showing off a rather underused British cheese.

Preheat the oven to 180°C/350°F/gas mark 4. Quarter the fennel and drizzle over the oil. Using half the butter, dab it over the fennel and season with salt and pepper. Cover with tin foil and bake until tender. Leave the oven on.

Wipe the mushrooms and sauté in the remaining butter until all the juices that have come out of them have evaporated. Add the thyme and more seasoning.

Whisk together the eggs and cream and season. Add half of the single Gloucester to the mix. Place the fennel and mushrooms in an ovenproof dish, pour over the egg and cream mixture and sprinkle over the remaining cheese. Bake for 20–25 minutes or until golden and almost firm. Sprinkle some fresh chopped parsley on top and serve.

serves 6

2 TBSP VEGETABLE OIL

1.5KG (3LB 5OZ) BONED LAMB
    SHOULDER, DICED INTO
    PIECES ABOUT 2CM/¾ INCH SQUARE

2 RED ONIONS, FINELY SLICED

LEAVES FROM A SPRIG OF ROSEMARY,
    FINELY CHOPPED

½ LEMON, WASHED AND DICED
    (SKIN ON WITH PIPS REMOVED)

250ML (9FL OZ) WHITE WINE

12 TOMATOES, PEELED AND
    ROUGHLY CHOPPED

SALT AND PEPPER

2 TSP CASTER SUGAR

ABOUT 1 LITRE (1¾ PINTS) LAMB STOCK

FOR THE SUET PASTRY

350G (12OZ) SELF-RAISING FLOUR

180G (6OZ) SUET

COLD WATER, IF NECESSARY

1 LARGE PUDDING BASIN
    (12CM/5 INCH DIAMETER)

evenlode lamb pudding

This pudding is named after the River Evenlode, which runs near the pub.

To make the suet pastry, mix the flour and suet together and knead till combined, adding water if necessary. Wrap in clingfilm and leave to rest while you make the filling. Heat the oil in a pan and brown the lamb pieces all over. Remove and place in a bowl. In the same pan, sweat the onions over a low heat until soft but not coloured. Add the rosemary and diced lemon and cook for 5 minutes. Add the wine and allow to reduce by half. Add the tomatoes and cook until they are soft, then put the lamb back in. Season well with salt, pepper and a little sugar. Put in enough stock to cover and simmer gently without a lid for at least 1 hour, or until the lamb is absolutely tender. Check the seasoning and leave to cool while you prepare the pastry.

Roll two-thirds of the pastry into a ball, and do the same with the remaining third. Roll the larger pastry ball to about 5mm/¼ inch thick, taking care not to overwork it. Lightly dust the pudding basin with flour then gently lift the pastry into the basin, allowing a small overlap over the edges. Roll the smaller ball to the same thickness. Fill the basin with the cooled lamb mixture, and cover with the top. Press the edges together until it is completely sealed. Wrap the pudding in heatproof clingfilm (or foil) all the way around.

Fill a large saucepan with enough water to come halfway up the pudding basin. Bring the water to a simmer, gently place the basin in and cover with a lid. Steam for 1 hour, checking occasionally that the water does not dry up. Preheat the oven to 200°C/400°F/gas mark 6.

To serve, carefully remove the clingfilm or foil, making sure you do not burn yourself, and place the basin in the oven for 5 minutes to slightly firm the edges. Remove from the oven and run a knife round the edges to loosen the pudding, place a plate over the top and turn upside down. This is great with purple sprouting broccoli, curly kale or cabbage.

serves 6
300ML (½ PINT) FULL FAT MILK
300ML (½ PINT) DOUBLE CREAM
100G (3½OZ) CASTER SUGAR
6 EGG YOLKS
150ML (5FL OZ) ELDERFLOWER CORDIAL

FOR THE RASPBERRY RIPPLE
100G (3½OZ) RASPBERRIES (FROZEN ONES CAN
BE USED IF FRESH AREN'T IN SEASON)
25G (1OZ) CASTER SUGAR
50ML (2FL OZ) ELDERFLOWER CORDIAL

elderflower & raspberry ice cream

Elderflower has the most gorgeous Muscat-like scent. It is usually paired with gooseberries but is also terrific with raspberries. Emily makes this with frozen raspberries when the fruit is out of season.

Bring the milk and cream to the boil with a tablespoon of the sugar. Beat the eggs and the remaining sugar together. Slowly pour the hot milk into the egg and sugar mix, stirring as you do so. Return this to a clean pan and cook very gently over a low heat. You must stir almost continuously and be careful not to let the mixture boil or it will scramble. You want to end up with a custard which is thick enough to coat the back of a spoon.

Take the custard off the heat and add the elderflower cordial. Pour through a sieve into a jug.

Blend the raspberries and sugar with a stick blender or in a food processor. Pass through a fine sieve into a saucepan. Bring this up to a gentle simmer and let it reduce to a syrupy consistency. Add the elderflower cordial and keep chilled.

Churn the base ice-cream in an ice-cream machine, or pour into a shallow container and freeze in the freezer, beating it 3 or 4 times during the freezing process to break down the crystals and make a smooth ice.

Scoop out the base ice-cream and, as you put it in a container to put in the freezer, stir in the raspberry and elderflower purée to get a ripple effect. Freeze.

the best of the rest

the devonshire arms

Lavish, opulent and luxurious are not words you might normally choose for a pub but they perfectly describe The Devonshire Arms. The place was always well known because of its proximity to Chatsworth House, but in 2006 the Duchess took it over and she has created a stylish and lovely place. There are tub chairs covered in bright candy striped fabric and funky bar stools, all sitting comfortably in among the old beams and exposed stone. Menus are clever, offering a good range of sensible classic pub food – ploughmans, grilled Chatsworth gammon, warm rice pudding with marmalade – plus more funky global dishes. You might find a salad made with tofu and asian leaves or Chatsworth lamb with chilli, coriander and potato curry, for example. A truly original place.

Devonshire Square, Beeley, Matlock, Derbyshire, DE4 2NR
Tel. 01629 733259, www.devonshirebeeley.co.uk
Serves lunch and dinner every day, rooms available.

the druid inn

A gorgeous old stone building set in beautiful countryside near Matlock. Unsuspecting diners might be surprised with the inn's interior – this is a very modern, glossy gastropub. The Thompson family who run it – mum, dad and two sons – have been determined to put the Druid on the culinary map and have even won awards for their sarnies (and who could resist a sandwich of ribeye steak with caramelised onions and stilton?). The food is at its best here when it's simple. A pint of prawns, chicken liver parfait and black pudding with crispy bacon and brown-sauce onions all hit the spot. And all of it can be eaten in the bar with its old tiled floor or any of the dining areas (all pale wood and minimalist décor). The beers on offer are from the Leatherbritches brewery.

Main Street, Birchover, Matlock, Derbyshire, DE4 2BL
Tel. 01629 650302, www.thedruidinn.co.uk
Serves lunch and dinner every day.

the three horseshoes

A corker. Ian Davison and Jennie Ison took over The Three Horseshoes – formerly a farriers – in 2005 and have worked wonders with the place. They've given the small bar a new lease of life without spoiling it in any way. It is a beautiful space with quarry tile floors, a big fireplace with a rough-hewn wooden surround and little tables with iron work legs. And then there are the dining areas with their sisal matting, highly polished old tables and eclectic prints. People come for the food as well as the environment. The menu is unashamedly brasserie style, full of classics such as bacon and poached egg salad, chicken liver parfait and lamb shanks with mustard mash. The only niggle is the fusing of dishes from different parts of the world, not always to best effect (witness beef in Cajun spices served with Greek tzatziki). Don't miss the spectacular Victorian bar counter, bought before the owners purchased The Three Horseshoes and carefully kept until the right home was found.

Breedon-on-the-Hill, Derbyshire, DE73 8AN
Tel. 01332 695129, www.thehorseshoes.com
Serves lunch every day and dinner (except Sunday).

the bell at sapperton

Very Cotswolds, very smart country – there is even a tethering rail outside where you can leave your horse. It caters to a well-heeled crowd who come for the wine (good list) and the well-sourced food. Dishes are chalked up on a blackboard above the fireplace and are crowd pleasers: local pigeon, rare-breed meats and fish from Cornwall are all well handled. Sensibly a different 'pub classic' – cottage pie or fish and chips – is served on particular days of the week, and then there are more upmarket options such as confit of duck leg with ginger, chilli and plum sauce or smoked venison with roast figs and orange. The food is better when it stays the right side of complicated. The dining areas, on several levels, have modern art on the bare stone walls and are brimming with fresh flowers. Eminently civilized.

Sapperton, Cirencester, Gloucestershire, GL7 6LE
Tel. 01285 760298, www.foodatthebell.co.uk
Serves lunch and dinner every day.

the butchers arms

The Butcher's Arms shows what's great about the evolution of British dining pubs. Chef and owner James Winter has cooked in some of the finest restaurants in Britain – Marwick's in Bristol and the Three Chimneys on the Isle of Skye to name two. But he eschewed a future in Michelin-starred eateries in favour of opening this pub in a tangle of lanes on the edge of Worcestershire. James and his wife (she does front of house) wanted to open a place where they could do everything themselves and become part of a small community. The red-brick building is charming and rickety, with a row of weathered stone toadstools in front. The inside redefines the term 'spare'. And the food is stunning: there's sweet and soothing turnip soup (yes, turnip), duck breast with a little fig tart and a sensational marmalade sponge pudding with Drambuie custard. The treacle tart, with its layer of puréed apple, is knock-out, too. Worth a detour? Worth schlepping up the motorway for, to be honest.

Lime St, Eldersfield, Gloucestershire, GL19 4NX Tel. 01452 840381, www.thebutchersarms.net Serves lunch and dinner every day.

the falcon inn

There's interesting food at this eternally popular Cotswold dining pub. The dishes are mainly British but not the usual suspects. There might be a ballotine of organic salmon with Lechlade crayfish and a celeriac and horseradish salad, a tart of slow roasted Dexter shin of beef with a poached duck egg and béarnaise or, more traditionally, Peashell Farm pork with parsnip purée, red cabbage and Bramley apple compote. The place also has a great buzzy atmosphere – partly due to the open kitchen which faces the dining area – though this doesn't ruin the pubby feel of the bar. There's a good selection of wines by the glass and decent guest beers as well.

London Road, Poulton, Cirencester, Gloucestershire, GL7 5HN, Tel. 01285 850844, www.thefalconpoulton.co.uk Serves lunch (every day) and dinner (except Sunday).

the baker's arms

An idyllic 16th-century thatched cottage is home to The Baker's Arms, an exemplary dining pub in the pretty village of Thorpe Langton. It shows a woman's touch – a warren of cute small rooms are kitted out with cottagey furnishings, prints and knick-knacks, settles and pews – and indeed chef-patron Kate Hubbard devotes herself to the place. Note the opening hours: this is a foodie pub more than a drinker's pub. That said, you can still pitch up for a pint and the place certainly feels pubby. Dishes are intensely flavoured and elegantly presented. The blackboard menu might offer scallops with black pudding, steak with a stilton and horseradish crust or duck with red pepper and ginger marmalade. Be sure to book – it's not always easy to get a table.

Main Street, Thorpe Langton, Market Harborough, Leicestershire, LE16 7TS, Tel. 01858 545201 www.thebakersarms.co.uk. Serves lunch on Saturday and Sunday and dinner Tuesday–Saturday.

the fox and hounds

A good solid-looking four-square pub in chic Knossington, Brian Baker and his sister Claire have, after refurbishment, maintained the place as a good popular local and drawn a crowd from further afield for the food. Brian, who mans the stoves, sources quality ingredients and then lets them speak for themselves. This is simple, carefully prepared food – and that is harder to turn out than you might think. Mostly the food is a mixture of British and French dishes – chilled watercress and potato soup, chicken with tarragon cream sauce, calves liver with champ – but the odd bit of contemporary global cookery turns up, such as scallops with crème fraîche and chilli dressing, a dish made famous by Kiwi chef, Peter Gordon. Dining is either in the bar or the dining room, but neither seat that many, so book or turn up early.

6 Somerby Road, Knossington, Leicestershire, LE15 8LY Tel. 01664 454676. Serves lunch every day and dinner (except Sunday and Monday).

tollemache arms

This 19th-century inn has had a massive makeover and the result is a gracious, tasteful pub and restaurant. The food is the real draw. Chef Mark Gough previously worked at Le Manoir aux Quat' Saisons under Raymond Blanc and at Hambleton Hall in Rutland. And his pedigree shows in every dish. First of all in the menu itself (modern British food with lots of Mediterranean leanings), which is clear and devoid of embellishment. What you see listed is what you get. Secondly, in his sheer skill. Every dish is polished and sourcing is obviously good. There might be pigeon breast on toast with onion marmalade, Shetland scallops with smoked bacon or rump of local venison with roast butternut squash. Desserts are what you might expect – lemon tart et al. – though with a few welcome fireworks (raspberry vodka champagne milkshake anyone?).

48 Main Street, Buckminster, Lincolnshire, NG33 5SA
Tel. 01476 860007, www.thetollemachearms.com
Serves lunch (except Monday) and dinner (except Sunday and Monday), rooms available.

boar's head

This is still very much a local, but chef-patron Bruce Buchan nevertheless turns out ambitious cooking and attracts food lovers from all over the place. His style is modern and bold. You can choose from foie gras with brioche and rhubarb, Cornish scallops, red mullet with ratatouille and chorizo, or venison with mustard sauce. His sourcing is impeccable – lamb and pork are reared locally, game comes from Lockinge Estate and the fruit and veg are, as far as possible, within striking distance of the pub. Fish from Newlyn makes a strong presence. Bruce makes his own bread daily so it's good to pitch up at lunchtime when the various loaves are hot from the oven.

Church Street, Ardington, Wantage, Oxfordshire
OX12 8QA
Tel. 01235 833254, www.boarsheadardington.co.uk
Serves lunch and dinner every day, rooms available.

the fox and hounds

A smart but still very much traditional pub, it is the food that draws people to this 15th-century flint-and-brick cottage. Owned by Brakspears but with Kieron Daniels as the chef-landlord, you'll find strong, bold, earthy cooking. Scandinavian cured herrings with horseradish cream, beef hash with a fried egg and Gressingham duck breast with apples and a potato gratin, mussel and shrimp risotto and panettone bread-and-butter pudding all make regular appearances. The restaurant part of the operation has an open kitchen so you can watch the action while supping your pint and developing your appetite.

Christmas Common, Watlington, Oxfordshire, OX49 5HL
Tel. 01491 612599. Serves lunch and dinner daily.

the king's head inn

I was tipped off so often about this place that I was almost – perversely – reluctant to go. It's the kind of place you fall in love with, small and cottagey on the outside, with a beguiling cobbled courtyard and set in the gorgeous village of Bledington with its duck pond and perfect green. Co-owner Nic Orr-Ewing has overseen the interior and created lovely rooms full of eclectic bits of furniture. The bar is traditional, complete with richly glowing wooden bar stools and the dining areas are smart with polished tables and rich fabrics. Husband Archie is very popular with everyone (I have never heard so many people return from a pub knowing the owner's name). Food is good, straightforward stuff, carefully cooked and delivered without tricksy presentation. Comfort is key – there might be potted shrimps, steak and ale pie and Aberdeen Angus beef fillet from Archie's uncle's nearby farm.

The Green, Bledington, Oxfordshire, OX7 6XQ
Tel. 01608 658365, www.kingsheadinn.net
Serves lunch and dinner every day, rooms available.

the trout at tadpole bridge

The Trout was in my last book but a change of ownership and some refurbishing meant another look. And no wonder it has been getting rave reviews. The original interior – pale stone walls and tiled floors – has been retained but it is now filled with smart chairs (no uncomfortable spindle-backs here) and highly polished wooden tables. The effect is one of rural luxury. And the food is knock-out. You'll find both the posh and the prosaic on the menu – loin of venison with smoked pancetta and salardaise potatoes or fish and chips with tartare sauce – all done very well. And if you like sausages, you should buy a house nearby. They do speciality sausages as part of their 'Sausage Club' every Thursday. Merguez with garlicky sweet potato mash and salsa verde, venison bangers with caramelized onions and horseradish mash, black pudding with crispy bacon and…well…you get the picture. They also suggest the perfect beer or wine to go with each sausage. Heaven.
**Buckland Marsh, Faringdon, Oxfordshire, SN7 8RF
Tel. 01367 870382, www.troutinn.co.uk
Serves lunch every day and dinner (except Sunday), rooms available.**

the jackson stops inn

It's a great name – when the pub was once for sale, the estate agent's sign was up so long outside the pub that the name stuck – and a lovely place. Owner Richard Graham has two other good pubs as well, The Collweston Slater (he seems to specialise in eccentrically named pubs) and The Old Pheasant at Glaston, but this is probably the jewel in the crown. An old thatched building with a tiny and spare bar and a selection of rambling rooms, it is both a popular village local and a draw for foodies. The food is sensible country fare for the most part – pork belly with cider sauce and venison with dumplings and celeriac are the kinds of things you'll find on a sensibly short and frequently changed menu. Puds are a particular highlight.
**Rookery Lane, Stretton, Rutland, LE15 7RA
Tel. 01780 410237. Serves lunch (except Monday) and dinner (except Sunday and Monday).**

crown country inn

A handsome Tudor inn – it's been a courtroom in the past – the Crown is a shrine to local food producers and farmers. Maps and information about the inn's suppliers cover the walls and chef-patron Richard Arnold cares passionately about them. The menu is a total celebration of local grub: you can have little toasts of black pudding with Wenlock Edge bacon, confit of Breckland duck with mushed peas and roast onions or chicken – which they smoke themselves – with mustard creamed leeks. Cheeses are great – a treat if you like to discover lesser-know British gems such as Hereford hop. Foodie Ludlow is, of course, on the doorstep.
**Munslow, Nr. Craven Arms, Shropshire, SY7 9ET
Tel. 01584 841205, www.crowncountryinn.co.uk
Serves lunch (except Sunday) and dinner (until 7:30pm on Sunday and closed Monday), rooms available.**

the inn at farnborough

Chef-patron Anthony Robinson and his wife Johanna put their heart and soul into this place. Formerly a pretty run-down inn, they refurbished it, changed the name and gave it a whole new lease of life. It's as neat as a pin, less rambling and more elegant than most pubs and, with walls in a warm ochre colour, utterly relaxing. Anthony serves up classy food that has local and seasonal written all over it. And as it encompasses British, Italian and French dishes it has something for everyone: shellfish bisque (for which they are famous), pork with bubble and squeak, apples and calvados and seafood linguine. There's a Great British Classics section on the menu which features fish cakes et al. (and a cracking beef and Hook Norton ale stew) and even side dishes are considered – chips with aïoli, pea and mint purée or Mediterranean vegetable gratin to name just a few. Staff are supremely professional and there are lovely gardens to eat in when the sun shines.
**Farnborough, Nr. Banbury, Warwickshire, OX17 1DZ
Tel. 01295 690615, www.innatfarnborough.co.uk
Serves lunch and dinner every day.**

east of england

The Hole in the Wall is so tucked away you could easily get lost looking for it – though the smell of their humungous steak and onion sandwiches may lead you there by the nose.

Christopher Leeton and Jenny Lee – he cooks, she does front of house – were previously at the helm at The Loughpool Inn in Herefordshire (owned by ex-restaurateur Stephen Bull, though it's now been sold on) then decided to come home to Cambridgeshire. Bull backed them, and since opening in 2005 they have breathed new life into The Hole in the Wall, making it once again the focal point of the village.

A low 15th-century hostelry painted in cream, with black beams and pots full of lavender and nasturtiums, it looks every inch the perfect English country pub. Horse brasses, copper pans and dried hops make the inside refreshingly old-fashioned – and so is the spirit of the place. There are plenty of drinkers nursing pints (they have a good range of real ales from Norfolk, Suffolk and Cambridgeshire) and the menu pays homage to great old English stalwarts such as beef and ale pie, toad-in-the-hole, shoulder of mutton and plum crumble, as well as more modern dishes such as bream with cucumber, dill and brown-shrimp butter.

Christopher has done his time in dining pubs but started out under Shaun Hill at the country house hotel, Gidleigh Park. Both he and Jenny have always felt more at home in pubs, however. 'I want to be able to say hello and goodbye to everyone who comes in,' says Jenny. 'Stephen Bull taught us how not to run a place like a restaurant, to be more laid back and not skip around asking diners if they were okay.' They also wanted to become part of a community as well as cooking for one. Much of the produce used here comes from local gardeners. Sourcing is everything to Chris. He was tracking down the best suppliers before they'd even closed the deal on the pub, and suppliers get top billing on the menu.

The only occasional frustration, and it is one echoed by other pub chefs, is the reluctance of diners to try more old-fashioned dishes and to be happy with plainer presentation. 'I like to try old-fashioned dishes but that doesn't always work,' says Chris. 'I love faggots but they just didn't go here. I think people feel a bit cheated when they get something as ordinary as crumble – even when it's great crumble. They don't necessarily want to eat what they can eat at home.' Thank goodness he keeps trying, though. If you feel like food that isn't gussied up but is prepared with care, this is the place to go.

the hole in the wall

2 HIGH STREET, LITTLE WILBRAHAM, CAMBRIDGESHIRE, CB1 5JY • TEL 01223 812282 • www.the-holeinthewall.com
SERVES LUNCH (EXCEPT MONDAY) AND DINNER (EXCEPT SUNDAY AND MONDAY)

serves 8

FOR THE HAM STOCK

1 HAM HOCK

1 CARROT

1 ONION, HALVED

2 CELERY STICKS

2 STAR ANISE

4 CLOVES

2 BAY LEAVES

2 CLOVES GARLIC, CRUSHED

1 TBSP CORIANDER SEEDS

1 TBSP MUSTARD SEEDS

1 TBSP JUNIPER BERRIES

FOR THE SOUP

75G (2½OZ) BUTTER

2 ONIONS, ROUGHLY CHOPPED

2 CLOVES GARLIC, CRUSHED

300G (10½OZ) YELLOW SPLIT PEAS,
  SOAKED IN COLD WATER FOR 12 HOURS

200ML (7FL OZ) SINGLE CREAM

FRESHLY GROUND BLACK PEPPER

FOR THE CREAM

1 SMALL BUNCH OF CHIVES, CHOPPED

FRESHLY GROUND BLACK PEPPER

100ML (3½FL OZ) WHIPPING CREAM,
  LIGHTLY WHIPPED

yellow split pea soup with flaked ham & chive cream

A soup to warm the cockles of your heart.

Put the ham hock in a heavy-based pan, cover with cold water and bring to the boil. Simmer for 10 minutes then remove from the pan. Put the hock in another pan with all the other ingredients for the stock and cover with cold water. Bring to the boil then turn the heat down and simmer on a medium heat for 3 hours, until the meat falls off the bone easily. Remove the hock and strain the stock. Rinse the saucepan.

To make the soup, put the butter in the saucepan and sweat the onions and garlic for 15 minutes or until the onions are soft but not coloured. Add the drained split peas and 600ml (1 pint) of the ham stock. Bring to the boil then turn down to a simmer and cook for 30–40 minutes or until the peas are completely soft. Remove from the heat and leave to cool. Purée in a blender, add the single cream and season with black pepper, to taste.

To serve, flake the flesh from the ham hock. Warm the soup without boiling it. Mix the chives and some black pepper with the lightly whipped cream. Scatter some of the flaked ham and a spoonful of the cream over each serving.

'The Hole in the Wall is so tucked away you could easily get lost looking for it – though the smell of their humungous steak and onion sandwiches may lead you there by the nose.'

serves 4

4TBSP OIL

12 TOP-QUALITY PORK SAUSAGES

1 LARGE EGG

2TBSP CHOPPED FRESH THYME

SALT AND PEPPER

600ML (1 PINT) MILK

225G (8OZ) PLAIN FLOUR

FOR THE ONION GRAVY

4TBSP OIL

3 ONIONS, FINELY SLICED

1TBSP TOMATO PURÉE

500ML (18FL OZ) STRONG BEEF STOCK

SALT AND PEPPER

toad-in-the-hole with onion gravy

It's important to get really top-quality sausages for this dish, and to heat the fat – as with Yorkshire pudding – till it is almost smoking.

Heat half the oil in a frying pan and brown the sausages all over – you don't want to cook them through, just to give them a good colour. Whisk the egg with the thyme, salt and pepper and half the milk. Gradually add the flour and mix to a smooth paste. Add the rest of the milk. Preheat the oven to 210°C/420°F/gas mark 7.

For the onion gravy, heat the oil in a heavy-based frying pan over a medium-low heat and sauté the onions until soft and brown. This can take as long as 15 minutes. Add the tomato purée and the beef stock and cook for 5 minutes. Season with salt and pepper. Set aside until you want to serve.

Heat the remaining 2tbsp oil in a large roasting tin until it is very, very hot. Add the sausages and pour the pudding batter over them. Immediately put into the oven and bake for 20–25 minutes until the batter is puffed and golden. Do not open the oven door during this time (if you have an oven with a window, peek through it) or the rising batter will collapse.

Serve with mash and hot onion gravy. Roast carrots or braised red cabbage go well on the side.

serves 8

3 TBSP VEGETABLE OIL

1.5 KG (3 LB 5 OZ) BEEF CHUCK, CUT
  INTO 5 CM (2 INCH) CUBES

2 LARGE ONIONS

½ TBSP TOMATO PURÉE

LEAVES FROM 2 SPRIGS OF THYME

2.5 LITRES (4½ PINTS) BEEF STOCK

SALT AND PEPPER

4 LARGE FLAT FIELD
  MUSHROOMS, SLICED

2 TBSP WORCESTERSHIRE SAUCE

1.2 LITRES (2 PINTS) ALE, SUCH
  AS WOODFORDE'S WHERRY

500 G (1 LB 2 OZ) SHORTCRUST PASTRY

2 EGGS, BEATEN, FOR THE GLAZE

FOR THE HORSERADISH CREAM

100 ML (3½ FL OZ) WHIPPING CREAM

4 TBSP HORSERADISH CREAM

FRESHLY GROUND BLACK PEPPER

beef & wherry ale pie with horseradish cream

Wherry ale is brewed in Norfolk by Woodforde's so Chris likes to use that
but any other ale will do. I'd never thought of doing a horseradish cream
with a beef pie. It's an inspired addition.

Heat the oil in a heavy-based pan and brown the beef in batches, making sure you get a
good colour all over. Add the onions and cook until softening. Add the tomato purée, thyme,
beef stock and salt and pepper and bring the mixture to just under the boil. Turn the heat
down, cover the pan and cook over a very low heat for 1½ hours. Add the sliced mushrooms,
Worcestershire sauce and ale and cook for a further 40 minutes, or until the beef is tender.

Preheat the oven to 180°C/350°F/gas mark 4. Divide the beef and mushroom mix between
four pie dishes and brush the edges of the dishes with beaten egg. Roll out the pastry and cut
out pieces big enough to fit the top of each pie dish. Press the pastry on to the rim of the dishes
and cut off the excess. Crimp the edges with your fingers or the tines of a fork. If you like,
use the bits of leftover pastry to make decorations for the tops of the pies. Brush the pies with
the beaten egg and pierce the centre of each with a small sharp knife. Bake for 20 minutes,
or until golden brown.

Whip the cream and add the horseradish cream and pepper. Serve the pies with the sauce,
with some honey-roast carrots on the side.

serves 8–10

1 SHOULDER OF MUTTON, BONED, ROLLED AND
   TIED (ABOUT 3½–4KG/7LB 9OZ–9LB IN WEIGHT)
SALT AND PEPPER

FOR THE MINT SAUCE
1 BUNCH OF FRESH MINT
2TBSP CASTER SUGAR
4TBSP WHITE WINE VINEGAR

FOR THE CAPER SAUCE
250ML (9FL OZ) LAMB STOCK
100ML (3½FL OZ) CHICKEN STOCK
1 SPRIG OF ROSEMARY
20G (¾OZ) CAPERS, RINSED OF SALT OR BRINE

twelve hour slow-roast shoulder of mutton with mint & caper sauce

This is only worth doing for a crowd but it's a bit of an 'event' meal and guests will love it. It's one of the most popular Sunday lunch dishes at The Hole in the Wall.

Preheat the oven to 130°C/250°F/gas mark ½. Season the mutton and put it on a rack in a roasting tin. Prick the mutton all over with a skewer and cover with tin foil. Roast for 8 hours, basting every 30 minutes with the fat that runs off. After 8 hours, turn the oven down very slightly, remove the foil and cook for a further 4 hours, basting every hour. The joint will become brown and very soft.

To make the mint sauce, put the leaves in a food processor with the sugar and blend until fine, then add the vinegar and blend again. Chill immediately.

When the 12 hours of cooking has finished, remove the mutton from the roasting tin and pour off the fat and juices. Skim the fat off the juices (this is good to use for roast potatoes) and mix the cooking juices with the lamb and chicken stocks. Boil until reduced by half. Add the rosemary a few minutes before the end just to scent it. Strain and add the capers.

Remove the string from the shoulder of mutton. Serve the mutton with the cold mint sauce and the warm caper sauce, and with roast potatoes and carrots on the side.

serves 6

1KG (2LB 4OZ) PLUMS, HALVED
   AND STONED
200G (7OZ) CASTER SUGAR
PINCH OF GROUND CINNAMON
200ML (7FL OZ) SWEET WHITE WINE
250G (9OZ) UNSALTED BUTTER, DICED

FOR THE CRUMBLE TOPPING
250G (9OZ) COLD UNSALTED BUTTER
120G (4OZ) PLAIN FLOUR

120G (4OZ) JUMBO OATS
FINELY GRATED RIND OF 2 LEMONS
50G (1¾OZ) SOFT DARK BROWN
   SUGAR

FOR THE CUSTARD
150ML (¼ PINT) MILK
150ML (¼ PINT) DOUBLE CREAM
1 VANILLA POD, SPLIT
8 EGG YOLKS
70G (2½OZ) CASTER SUGAR

plum crumble with proper custard

Despite the plethora of pannacotta and tiramisu on pub menus, it is often the old-fashioned English puds that seem most fitting.

Place the halved and stoned plums in a heavy-based pan, add the sugar, cinnamon, white wine and butter and cover. Cook over a medium heat until the plums are soft, but not mushy. Remove and strain. Save the juices.

To make the crumble, put the butter, flour, oats and lemon rind in a bowl and rub together until the mixture comes together to form little lumps.

Preheat the oven to 170°C/325°F/gas mark 3. Put the plums and their cooking juices into a buttered ovenproof dish and spread the crumble mixture on top. Sprinkle over the brown sugar and bake until golden brown.

To make the custard, put the milk and cream into a saucepan. Scrape the seeds out of the vanilla pod with a small knife and put these and the pod into the saucepan. Heat together until boiling. Immediately take the pan off the heat and leave to infuse for 30 minutes.

Mix the egg yolks and sugar together and beat until pale. Remove the vanilla pod and pour the milk and cream mixture on to the eggs, stirring as you do so. Put the mixture back into the pan and cook on a very low heat, stirring continuously, until the mixture thickens. Do not let it boil or the mixture will curdle. Serve the crumble with the custard.

the best of the rest

the crown inn

A pub so loved by the locals that they saved it from being turned into a private dwelling in 2001, The Crown is the focal point of village life in pretty Broughton, though it's not a cosy, trad refuge. The inside is filled with light, pale wood and terra cotta tiles. Simon Cadge's food is sensible, unshowy and very good indeed. He sends out the kind of dishes which make for perfect pub dining: Irish black pudding with mash, spinach and tomato chutney (who wouldn't go out of their way for that?), smoked haddock fishcakes with grain mustard sauce and, for pud, lemon posset. There are great lawns at the back for summer lounging and sunning.

Bridge Road, Broughton, Huntingdon, Cambridgeshire PE28 3AY, Tel. 01487 824428.
www.thecrownbroughton.co.uk
Serves lunch and dinner (except Monday and Tuesday).

the cock

Enterprising owners Oliver Thain and Richard Bradley (they own two other watering holes – see them on the website below) have done great things with this place. They manage to make it both a welcoming local and a swish eatery. The bar is utterly simple – almost spare – with plain boards, a wood-burner and settles. The creamy coloured dining room is equally uncluttered. Pub and brasserie classics abound: sausages (the chef makes his own) and mash, duck parcels with sweet and sour cucumber and wild mushroom risotto. There's a fab cheese board as well.

47 High Street, Hemingford Grey, Huntingdon, Cambridgeshire, PE28 9BJ
Tel. 01480 463609, www.cambscuisine.com
Serves lunch and dinner every day.

the headley

It can be difficult when really high-end chefs start going down the gastropub route and slightly makes me dread eating their 'simpler' fare. Will it really be simpler or will it be posh fish and chips with some kind of foam, a 'cappuccino' of mushy peas? The chef here, Daniel Clifford, has two Michelin stars at Midsummer House in Cambridge, but he manages to make the leap to pub – most of the time.

The foams come with the pudding. But before that you can have plenty of gutsy, modern pubby offerings: calves liver with smoked bacon, duck confit and steak and kidney pie. Does your heart good to read the menu. The place needs to be more lived in; everything is a bit too pristine. But let's not gripe. We're lucky that chefs of his calibre want to cook in more democratic eateries. Especially when they can control the foams.

The Common, Great Warley, Brentwood, Essex, CM13 3HS Tel. 01277 216104, www.theheadley.co.uk. Serves lunch (except Monday) and dinner (except Sunday and Monday).

the mistley thorn

A neat-as-a-pin hostelry in a smart Essex village. Owner Sherri Singleton also runs a cookery school next door and injects the place with verve and energy. Fish is one of the best things here: chowder, fishcakes, mussels, home-cured salmon and big tranches of roast cod are all spot-on. And the chips are fab. The pub feels more like a tasteful club than country local – there are Conran-style rattan chairs and sharp modern tables – but it still gets treated as a pub, albeit a smart one.

High Street, Mistley, Colchester, Essex, CO11 1HE Tel. 01206 392821, www.mistleythorn.co.uk
Serves lunch and dinner every day, rooms available.

the sun inn

This is a very special place: a taste of Italy in a pretty corner of Essex. Chef and owner Piers Baker does terrific unfussy Med food – especially Italian dishes – that are delivered as if from mamma's kitchen (plain white plates, no fuss). You'll want everything on the menu: steak with cannellini beans, squash and fresh horseradish (yes, they eat horseradish in northern Italy), stinco di vitello, (shin of veal roasted with red wine vinegar, tomatoes, spring garlic and capers) and coscia d'agnello ai ferri (chargrilled leg of lamb with salsa di erbe). The wine list is a fantastic read, too, and much of the food is sourced locally. The Sun is also very handsome: painted a beguiling deep ochre and with a rambling layout, glossy dark wooden floors and timbered Tudor ceilings. Piers' wife runs a small shop next door – Victoria's Plums – selling local fruit and veg. A great place for Londoners looking for Sunday lunch in the country without going too far.

High Street, Dedham, Colchester, Essex, CO7 6DF
Tel. 01206 323351, www.thesuninndedham.com
Serves lunch and dinner every day, rooms available.

the king's head hotel

It may be a grand Victorian pile but The King's Head is übercool and nothing like a trad local. Expect suede sofas, a bar with a swish metal counter and tricksy lighting. And the food is very good. Chef Neil Rutland takes advantage of great local ingredients – you might find Thornham oysters done three ways (natural, with vodka and chilli granita and in Adnam's beer batter), dressed crab or cod with brown shrimp and dill butter sauce. There's a good mixture of reassuringly English dishes (kedgeree and fishcakes, for example) as well as 'global' takes on other ones.

Great Bircham, Kings Lynn, Norfolk PE31 6RJ
Tel. 01485 578265, www.the-kings-head-bircham.co.uk
Serves lunch and dinner every day, rooms available.

the anchor

The gorgeous little village of Walberswick is now achingly hip so the London-on-Sea trendies who escape here must be thrilled that Mark Dorber (former landlord of The White Horse in London's Parson's Green) and his wife, Sophie, have brought such energy to this Adnams boozer. The food is much less 'gastro' than the stuff offered in other pubs in this book but it is good simple grub, done very well. Expect a sweet, more-ish bowlful of Irish stew in the winter and barbecued meat on the vast lawn in the summer. As in Mark's London pub, there are choices of beer to match the food.

Main Street, Walberswick, Suffolk, IP18 6UA
Tel. 01502 722112, www.anchoratwalberswick.com
Serves lunch and dinner every day, rooms available.

the bildeston crown

This ancient inn (it was built in 1529) has been given a glossy makeover and could now only be described as luxurious (especially the bedrooms). It still feels like a pub – there are wooden floors and ancient beams and the smell of burning logs fills the air – but gilt-framed mirrors, oil paintings and smart leather chairs put it most definitely in the chic bracket. The food, from chef-patron Chris Lee, is very good indeed and you can choose from classic dishes – herring roes on toast, English snails with garlic and parsley butter – or more unusual ones such as wild garlic risotto. Eat either in the bar (and it's a beautiful one – elegant but still cosy) or the smart dining room.

High Street, Bildeston, Suffolk, IP7 7EB
Tel. 01449 740510, www.thecrownbildeston.com
Serves lunch and dinner every day, rooms available.

the star inn

This is a little bit of Spain in the most English of pubs. Chef-patron is Maria Teresa Axon from Catalonia and as soon as you open the front door the smell of garlic, fish and olive oil subsumes you. She's particularly keen on fish – roast, grilled and in a terrific piscine stew. There are British dishes as well – venison in port and trad puddings – and also very English activities – games of darts and dominoes are always on the go. It's a snug little place with small rooms, low beams and warm fires, it dates from 1588 and is incredibly pretty. In summer the smell of flowers around the front win out over the aromas of Spain.

The Street, Lidgate, Bury St Edmunds, Suffolk, CB8 9PP
Tel. 01638 500275
Serves lunch and dinner every day (except Sunday).

the westleton crown

As it's near trendy Walberswick you have to get here early – it's very popular – or better still, book one of the fabulous rooms upstairs so you can be the first person at the bar. Food is best described as classically English with a bit of French flair. You'll get warm smoked salmon with sauce vierge, warm salt-cured haddock or a platter of local pork (including a rather wonderful Scotch egg). Despite the expensive makeover it has undergone, the place still exudes warmth and has masses of pubby character. There are flagstone floors, snug corners, beams, pews and warm fires. Lovely.

The Street, Westleton, Nr. Southwold, Suffolk, IP17 3AD
Tel. 01728 648777, www.westletoncrown.co.uk
Serves lunch and dinner every day, rooms available.

the gin trap inn

Despite the plough-shares above the front door, The Gin Trap is very much a dining pub in the smart contemporary vein. And it's popular and buzzy – tourists, well-heeled families and lunching ladies all beat a path to its door to eat local oysters, seafood chowder or duck confit with a beetroot and shallot dressing. Eat in the bar, restaurant or, in good weather, the lovely walled garden. Despite its trendiness, The Gin Trap maintains classic pubby elements and in winter you can enjoy sitting by a blazing log fire under ceilings of low black beams.

6 High Street, Ringstead, Hunstanton, Norfolk, PE36 5JU Tel. 01485 525264, www.gintrapinn.co.uk Serves lunch and dinner every day, rooms available.

the globe inn

This old coaching inn, right on the green, has been renovated by the owners of the trendy Victoria at the Holkham and they've fixed the place up with considerable style. There's an eclectic mix of new and old furniture, a wood-burning stove and cool lighting. It feels welcoming, despite the hipness, and the straightforward food is served in two bars and a dining room. Dishes such as lemon sole, Norfolk game (you'll get venison and partridge from the Holkham estate), wholetail scampi and decent steaks are delivered without any nonsense. Sunday lunch is a splendid, happy affair. Great beaches nearby too.

The Buttlands, Wells-Next-the-Sea, Norfolk, NR23 1EU Tel. 01328 710206, www.globeatwells.co.uk Serves lunch and dinner every day, rooms available.

the orange tree

Yet another smart and sophisticated Norfolk watering hole, The Orange Tree looks fairly ordinary on the outside but inside it's all contemporary neutrals – sisal flooring, pale wood and fireplaces stuffed with chunky logs – and there's a happy, affluent crowd of diners. There's even a trendy children's play area: no naff old climbing frames here. You can eat at the bar or in the dining room from a menu that lists nearly every gastropub and brasserie classic you can think of. Crispy pork belly, top-notch cheeseburgers and beer battered hake with minted peas are all delivered with aplomb.

High Street, Thornham, Hunstanton, Norfolk, PE36 6LY Tel. 01485 512213, www.theorangetreethornham.co.uk Serves lunch and dinner every day (food available until 6pm on Sunday), rooms available.

the walpole arms

If only this book could have been longer, The Walpole would have been up there with the leading entries. A truly lovely place (it looks like the kind of perfectly proportioned storybook house that children always draw) you will be utterly seduced by the twinkling lights which adorn it, and the garden. And its attractions don't stop there. Chef Andrew Parle used to be head chef at Alastair Little's Frith Street restaurant in London and he has as much talent as his mentor. The food is mostly Mediterranean. There are some classic Little dishes on the menu, such as his Chicken Orvieto, and the chicken liver parfait and fish soup are among the best you will ever taste. A gem.

The Common, Itteringham, Norwich, Norfolk, NR11 7AR Tel. 01263 587258, www.thewalpolearms.co.uk Serves lunch and dinner (except Sunday).

wales

All the chefs in this book talk about their locale with warmth, but especially the chef-proprietor at The Hardwick, Stephen Terry. Stephen first came to Wales as co-owner and chef of the legendary Walnut Tree Inn when Franco Taruschio handed over the reigns, and so immersed himself in the local community that he just didn't want to leave. He married a Welsh girl (and, as he puts it, 'her huge Welsh family'), and opened The Hardwick, a big, white, sensible-looking roadside pub. 'God, I would never go back to London,' he laughs. 'On cool, misty mornings here I start the day off with a run and I spend my whole time waving at people.' He even finds suppliers while jogging around the country lanes. His duck hash used to be served with a free-range hen egg, until one day he ran past a farm and spied duck eggs for sale. They were on the menu by lunchtime.

The Hardwick's menu is huge because it does what Stephen designed it to do: be all things to all people. You can have ham and egg and chips, or pasta rotolo with roast squash, spinach and goat's cheese; a fabulous toasted sandwich of roast mushrooms and melting fontina cheese, or salmon with roast beetroot, smoked bacon and horseradish cream. The chips are chunky and triple-cooked and there are no fewer than ten top-notch British and Irish cheeses on offer. It is dream pub food.

Such dishes are a million miles away from the fare Stephen used to cook. When he worked in London, the name Stephen Terry was on every foodie's lips. Working at Marco Pierre White's and the Gavroche, he was widely regarded as the most talented chef of his generation, better than Ramsay and up there with White. I wondered if it was difficult to offer pub food after this kind of background. 'Oh I can do poncy if it's required,' he says. 'And I have done it, so there isn't anything to prove. But that style isn't right for here. At The Hardwick I get really good ingredients and let them speak for themselves. It might only be ham and egg and chips, but what great ham and egg and chips! I call it Ronseal cooking. It does exactly what it says on the tin.' The place now boasts a Michelin Bib Gourmand and Stephen's happy to have it, but he has no desire to start chasing stars.

The Hardwick really is a proper pub with gutsy food and a local and happy clientele. Stephen's nearest neighbour gets his pints for a special price (it never increases) and can order a steak even when it's not on the menu (because that's what he likes). Stephen Terry really is unusual. He is true to himself, ploughs his own furrow, does exactly what he wants. And he makes – bar none – the best ham, egg and chips I've ever tasted.

the hardwick

OLD RAGLAN ROAD, ABERGAVENNY, MONMOUTHSHIRE, NP7 9AA • TEL 01873 854220 • www.thehardwick.co.uk
SERVES LUNCH (EXCEPT MONDAY) AND DINNER (EXCEPT SUNDAY AND MONDAY)

serves 3–4

1 X 900G (2LB) LIVE COCK CRAB (OR A DRESSED ONE)
2TBSP MAYONNAISE
SALT AND PEPPER
LEMON JUICE
SOURDOUGH, SALAD AND LEMON WEDGES, TO SERVE

FOR THE DRESSING
1 SMALLISH RED CHILLI, SEEDS AND PITH REMOVED
  AND FINELY DICED
2 SMALL SHALLOTS, FINELY DICED
JUICE OF ½ UNWAXED LEMON
APPROX. 15 LEAVES EACH OF MINT, CORIANDER AND
  FLAT LEAF PARSELY, FINELY CHOPPED
100ML (3½FL OZ) GOOD EXTRA VIRGIN OLIVE OIL
SEA SALT, TO TASTE

fresh white devon crab meat on grilled sourdough with chilli, coriander, lemon & mayonnaise

The oriental flavours of chilli and coriander in this super crab sandwich go brilliantly with the sweet white meat. Stephen says you can use prepared crab, but he does not like the pasteurised kind.

Boil the crab for 10 minutes, or you can steam it for 10–12 minutes (Stephen prefers this method). Remove the white meat from the claws and legs, checking for any stray bits of shell, and refrigerate.

Remove the brown meat from the shell. Blitz in a small food processor and pass through a fine sieve. Combine with equal quantities of homemade or good quality shop-bought mayonnaise. Check the seasoning, add a few drops of unwaxed lemon juice and refrigerate.

To season the white crab meat, combine all the dressing ingredients and then mix with with the crab. Finish with a little crushed seasalt (Stephen uses Halen Môn, from Anglesea) to taste.

Serve the crab meat on a slice of freshly grilled or toasted sourdough bread. Serve the brown meat mayonnaise on the side with a small salad garnish.

'The menu at The Hardwick is huge – it takes the prize for having more things on it I wanted to eat than any other – because it does what Stephen designed it to do: "be all things to all people".'

serves 8

2 HAM HOCKS

1 CARROT

1 STICK OF CELERY, ROUGHLY DICED

1 CLOVE GARLIC, CRUSHED

1 BAY LEAF

1 SMALL ONION, PEELED AND CUT
INTO 4

PARSLEY STALKS

5 BREASTS OF SKINNED FREE-RANGE
CHICKEN

75G (2½OZ) SALTED BUTTER, PLUS
A LITTLE MORE FOR THE LEEKS

75G (2½OZ) PLAIN FLOUR

4 LEEKS

1 X 250G (9OZ) PACKET OF GOOD-
QUALITY PUFF PASTRY

1 EGG, BEATEN

1 BUNCH OF FLAT-LEAF PARSLEY,
FINELY CHOPPED

SALT AND PEPPER

homemade free-range chicken, ham & leek pie

Best pie I've eaten in a long time.

Soak the ham hocks overnight in cold water. Place in a pan and cover with 10cm (4 inches) cold water. Bring to the boil and skim off any froth or impurities. Turn down to simmer. Add the carrot, celery, garlic, bay leaf, onion and parsley stalks. Cook on low gas with the top covered by a circle of greaseproof paper for approximately 4 hours.

Now add the chicken breasts and cook for a further 16–18 minutes, or until the chicken is done. Remove the ham and chicken. Cover with clingfilm and allow to cool. Pass the stock through a sieve into a saucepan, cover and keep warm. Melt the butter in a heavy-based pan and add the flour slowly to make a roux. Cook for 3–4 minutes, stirring, then slowly add the stock. When the sauce has a consistency that coats the back of a spoon and is smooth, pass through a sieve to get rid of any lumps, and keep to one side.

Preheat the oven to 170°C/325°F/gas mark 3. Cut the leeks in half lengthways and wash thoroughly. Cut into dice. Cook in a little butter until just soft but still vibrant in colour. Remove, strain and cool. Roll out the puff pastry to approximately 0.5cm (⅛ inch) thick. Cut out the lid for the pie, using the serving dish as a guide. Brush with the beaten egg and allow to rest for 10 minutes, before cooking in the oven for 25 minutes.

Meanwhile, dice the ham and chicken to approximately thumbnail-size pieces and stir into the sauce with the cooked leeks and finely chopped flat-leaf parsley. Check the seasoning. To serve, heat the pie mix in a saucepan, place into dish and put the lid on top. Serve with either mash, new potatoes or chips, and even a salad, if you fancy.

serves 8

2.25KG (5LB) PORK BELLY

20G (¾OZ) PLAIN FLOUR

2 EGGS, BEATEN

BREADCRUMBS FOR COATING THE PORK
  BELLY PORTIONS

100ML (3½FL OZ) RAPESEED OIL

1 BULB OF FENNEL

3 UNWAXED LEMONS, 1 JUICED

100ML (3½FL OZ) EXTRA VIRGIN OLIVE OIL

20G (¾OZ) CAPERS

SALT AND PEPPER

crispy belly of gloucester old spot pork with fennel, amalfi lemon & capers

This is an astonishing dish. I practically wrote this book just so that Stephen Terry would give me the recipe. Sweet, salty, fatty, acidic, sharp – and then there's the interplay of textures. It's got everything. To my mind, this is one of Stephen Terry's triumphs.

First cook the pork belly. Preheat the oven to 120°C/240°F/gas mark ¼. Place the meat in a roasting tray and half cover with water. Place a sheet of greaseproof paper directly onto the top of the belly and then place tin foil over the top of the roasting tray and fold down the edges to seal the pork in. Cook in the oven for 8 hours. Carefully remove the belly from the cooking liquid and allow to cool slightly on a tray, fat-side up.

Then you need to deconstruct the belly, taking out the bone, skin, sinew and most of the fat, and reconstruct it as a flat piece of meat that will be about half the size of the original. When you first remove the skin from the belly, reserve the soft underbelly fat and put this between each layer of pork belly meat to keep it moist. When you have finished layering the pork together, wrap it tightly in clingfilm and allow to set in the fridge. This takes a minimum of 4 hours. Preheat the oven to 180°C/350°F/gas mark 4. Remove the pork from the clingfilm and cut into 8 equal portions. Pass each portion through flour, egg and breadcrumbs and shallow fry in rapeseed oil over a medium heat until golden brown all over. Now place on a tray and transfer to the oven to heat completely through. This should take about 5 minutes. Meanwhile, finely slice the fennel, discarding the core, and place into iced water to crisp. Finely chop the fennel leaf and reserve.

When hot, cut each belly portion in half lengthways and place on a serving plate. Garnish with the drained fennel and the leaf, dressed with the lemon juice and extra virgin olive oil. Sprinkle capers on each belly, season with sea salt and freshly ground black pepper and serve with a quarter of lemon.

serves 8

4 COOKED SAUSAGES

100ML (3½FL OZ) EXTRA VIRGIN
OLIVE OIL

100G (3½OZ) BLACK OLIVES, STONED
AND HALVED

2 RED PEPPERS, ROASTED, PEELED
AND SLICED

100G (3½OZ) ROCKET

200G (7OZ) FRESH GOAT'S CHEESE,
CRUMBLED

SALT AND PEPPER

FOR THE GNOCCHI

8 RED DESIREE POTATOES, TO PRODUCE
500G (1LB) COOKED, SIEVED POTATO

130G (4½OZ) PLAIN FLOUR, PLUS EXTRA
FOR DUSTING

1 EGG YOLK

70G (2½OZ) FINELY GRATED PARMESAN

100ML (3½FL OZ) OLIVE OIL

SALT

potato gnocchi with red pepper, fresh perroche goat's cheese, trealy farm sausage & rocket

This is one of Stephen's signature dishes. He uses a goat's cheese from Neal's Yard Dairies, but you could use any other goat's cheese as long as it isn't too firm. The sausage too comes from the terrific Welsh charcutier, Trealy's, but if you can't get hold of this, use the best quality sausage you can find.

To make the gnocci, preheat the oven to 190°C/375°F/gas mark 5. Prick the raw, washed potatoes all over and place on a tray covered in rock salt. Bake for approximately 2 hours, or until cooked. Put a large saucepan of salted water on to boil. Cut the potatoes in half and scoop out the cooked potato. Pass the potato through a fine sieve and weigh out 500g (1lb 2oz). Add the flour, egg yolk, Parmesan, olive oil, and salt. Mix by hand to gently bring together and form a soft dough. Shape this into a ball and cover with clingfilm rubbed with a little olive oil. Using about a quarter of the dough at a time, roll it out on a floured work surface into a long sausage about 2.5cm (1 inch) across. With a sharp, floured knife cut off pieces approximately 2.5cm (1 inch) in length and put on a lightly floured tray. Make sure your salted water is boiling, and have a large bowl of ice-cold water on hand. Gently tip the tray of gnocchi into the boiling water and wait for them all to float to the surface. Remove as quickly as possible with a slotted spoon. Plunge straight into the ice-cold water. Remove, drain, place on a lightly oiled tray and refrigerate.

Cut the sausages into slices 0.5cm (¼ inch) thick. Heat one third of the olive oil in a large frying pan and cook the sausage until golden brown. Have a small saucepan of boiling water ready to reheat the gnocchi. Add the black olives and red pepper to the frying pan and drop the gnocchi into the boiling water for 1 minute. Remove the gnocchi with a slotted spoon and add to the frying pan. Put all the ingredients from the pan into a mixing bowl. Add the rocket and goats cheese and carefully mix. Add the remaining olive oil and season with salt and freshly ground black pepper.

serves 8

LEFTOVER RARE BEEF (APPROXIMATELY 800G/1LB 12OZ)

FOR THE DRESSING

2 SPRIGS OF ROSEMARY

2 CLOVES GARLIC

8 SALTED ANCHOVY FILLETS, FINELY CHOPPED

300ML (10FL OZ) OLIVE OIL

ROCKET, OLIVE OIL, LEMON JUICE AND PARMESAN, TO SERVE

carpaccio of rare roast herefordshire beef on rocket with anchovy, garlic and rosemary dressing

This dish is often done poorly but Stephen has great Herefordshire beef at his disposal. Buy the best beef you can afford for this. As Stephen says, 'It is quite tricky to give an amount for the beef as the dish was created to use up the roast beef from Sunday. Just buy a bigger ribeye joint (or another joint if you prefer) for Sunday so you can make this dish the next day. Or indeed cook a whole ribeye if you are cooking for a larger number of people. The essential part of this dish is to cook the beef slowly. We cook it at 145°C/280°C/gas mark 1½ for about 2¼ hours. Then allow it to cool completely, wrap in clingfilm and refrigerate for a minimum of 6 hours.'

To make the dressing, pick the leaves off the rosemary sprigs and chop very finely. Finely chop the garlic and the anchovy fillets (Stephen likes to use Ortiz anchovies). Heat the olive oil and add the garlic and rosemary. Stir and do not allow to colour. Add the anchovies and then blitz in a liquidizer until you have a smooth, runny paste that you can drizzle over the meat. Allow to cool.

Slice the beef as thinly as possible by hand. Put the beef on the plates with rocket leaves dressed with a little olive oil and lemon juice (but do not add salt as the dressing is salty).

Dress the beef with the rosemary dressing and finely shave a little Parmesan over each plateful. You can serve this with a slice of grilled sourdough bread drizzled with olive oil.

serves 8

500ML (18FL OZ) DOUBLE CREAM

500ML (18FL OZ) MILK

1 SPLIT VANILLA POD

190G (7OZ) PUDDING RICE

110G (4OZ) CASTER SUGAR

FOR THE APPLE COMPOTE

4 LARGE BRAMLEY APPLES, PEELED, CORED
    AND CUT INTO 1CM (½ INCH) DICE

100G (3½OZ) CASTER SUGAR

FOR THE CRUMBLED SHORTBREAD

50G (1¾OZ) SOFT SALTED BUTTER

75G (2½OZ) PLAIN FLOUR

1⅓ TBSP CORNFLOUR

½ TSP BAKING POWDER

45G (1½OZ) CASTER SUGAR

SEA SALT

warm rice pudding with tredilion farm bramley apple compote & shortbread crumble

Rice pudding turns up on many gastropub menus and it's one of our most popular British puds, but it's good to find a version that has been given a little spin. The crumble is from Dan Leppard's shortbread recipe.

Bring the double cream, milk and vanilla pod to the boil. Add the pudding rice and sugar and simmer until just cooked (about 12–15 minutes).

To make the compote, put the diced apple and sugar in a pan over a medium heat until cooked but not a complete purée. Allow to cool.

To make the crumbled shortbread, preheat the oven to 130°C/250°F/gas mark ½. Combine all the ingredients to form a crumbled mixture. Spread the mixture out onto a baking sheet and bake for approximately 35 minutes. Remove and allow to cool.

To serve, heat the rice pudding and apple compote separately. Place next to each other on a plate or bowl and scatter the crumbled shortbread down the middle.

serves 10

100G (3½OZ) 70% COCOA SOLIDS
   DARK CHOCOLATE
125G (4½OZ) SALTED BUTTER
200G (7OZ) CASTER SUGAR
25G (1OZ) SOFT BROWN SUGAR
25G (1OZ) DARK SOFT BROWN SUGAR
2 EGGS
60G (2½OZ) COCOA POWDER
35G (1¼OZ) PLAIN FLOUR
50G (1¾OZ) 70% COCOA SOLIDS
   DARK CHOCOLATE
50G (1¾OZ) WHITE CHOCOLATE
50G (1¾OZ) MILK CHOCOLATE
35G (1¾OZ) PISTACHIOS
50G (1¾OZ) PECANS
50G (1¾OZ) TOASTED BLANCHED
   HAZELNUTS

50G (1¾OZ) TOASTED BLANCHED
   ALMONDS
75G (2½OZ) RAISINS

FOR THE TOFFEE SAUCE
25G (1OZ) SOFT BROWN SUGAR
25G (1OZ) DEMARERA SUGAR
100G (3½OZ) DARK SOFT BROWN SUGAR
175G DOUBLE CREAM
25G (1OZ) SALTED BUTTER

FOR THE ICE CREAM
600ML (20FL OZ) DOUBLE CREAM
600ML (20FL OZ) WHOLE MILK
10 EGG YOLKS
200G (7OZ) CASTER SUGAR
1 X 400G (14OZ) POT GOOD SEVILLE
   ORANGE MARMALADE

warm triple-chocolate brownie with seville orange marmalade ice cream

I've put the brownie in for choclate lovers, but the star of the show here is the ice cream. You'll want to eat it by the bucketful.

To make the ice cream, bring the cream and milk to the boil in one saucepan. Whisk together the yolks and sugar using a hand whisk or in a mixer. Add to the hot milk and cream and mix. Pass through a fine sieve into a bowl. Cover with clingfilm and allow to cool. Stir in the marmalade and churn in an ice-cream machine. Freeze for 12 hours.

Preheat the oven to 170°C/325°F/gas mark 3. Melt the chocolate in a bowl on a pan of boiling water and leave to cool slightly. Meanwhile, cream together the butter and sugars. Gradually beat in the eggs. Stir in the chocolate. Sift together the cocoa powder and flour and fold into the mixture. Chop the chocolate into small chunks. Fold the chocolate and nuts into the brownie mixture along with the raisins. Place on a baking tray lined with parchment paper and level out with a palette knife. Cook for 22 minutes and allow to cool. Cut into portions about 6cm (2½ inches) square.

To make the toffee sauce, put all the ingredients in a pan, bring to the boil, stirring and cool. Leave and then warm up until ready to use. To serve, warm the brownie in oven until just soft and serve with a little toffee sauce over and a big fat scoop of ice cream.

A dining pub run by two former AA inspectors with their wives manning the stoves may sound like a pitch for a sit-com, but there is no crockery being thrown at Y Polyn. It is a remarkably relaxing place, with much kissing and greeting in the bar and plenty of children running round the dining room on a Sunday lunchtime. All is presided over by an ebullient Scot and Y Polyn's co-owner, Mark Manson, and it would be hard to find a better host. He'll let you try any of the wines by the glass and then tout the rest of the bottle to other diners.

The pub was formerly a drinking den and before that a toll-house; the name means 'pole', perhaps a collectors' barrier to stop people before they paid their dues to cross the nearby bridge. Y Polyn now feels more like a farmhouse kitchen than anything else, albeit a smart one. It's a whitewashed building with leaded windows. Inside, the tongue-and-groove is the colour of putty, and there are whitewashed stone walls, terra cotta tiled floors and plenty of sisal matting. Piles of logs and several fires make it feel so cosy you wish they had bedrooms for guests upstairs.

The food is perfect for the setting. Chefs Maryann Wright and Susan Manson find it impossible to describe their style but the menu is like one you might find in a rural French bistro, comfortably interwoven with British dishes, and all using local ingredients. They make a classic fish soup with rouille (you'd be unlikely to find a better one in Marseilles), pork rillettes with chutney, coq au vin, fish pie, a superb treacle tart and a locally famous (and hand-churned) honey and almond ice-cream. The side vegetable dishes come to the table in big shallow dishes with huge spoons so that you can help yourself. The veg were the best I found while researching this book. They simply do everything well: dauphinoise potatoes, braised fennel, red cabbage – you'll get more than just a few well-cooked carrots or tender-stem broccoli.

Susan and Maryann's aim is to offer perfect versions of classic dishes rather than more complicated food. Needless to say, the saltmarsh lamb and Welsh Black beef are sourced locally, as is the pork, and the four of them have, for the last 18 months, raised some of their own animals and poultry, with notable success with pigs. Sewin (sea trout) comes from local coracle fishermen and the rest of the fish comes from Brixham with an overnight courier. And Mark's sourdough! Sour, yeasty, properly salty: it is near miraculous that someone is making bread this good in Britain and not charging a fortune for it.

The word 'genuine' kept coming into my head as I ate here. Everything is fitting, from the slate tablemats to the no-nonsense farmhouse-style napkins, the homemade piccalilli to the Welsh cheeses. 'We like the ordinary done very well,' says Mark. And that is exactly what they do here: superlatively.

y polyn

CAPEL DEWI, NANTGAREDIG, CARMARTHENSHIRE, SA32 7LH • 01267 290000 • www.ypolynrestaurant.co.uk
SERVES LUNCH AND DINNER (EXCEPT MONDAY)

serves 6

900G (2LB) MUTTON SHOULDER, CUT INTO
   1.5CM/½ INCH CHUNKS
4–5TBSP OLIVE OIL
2 LARGE WHITE ONIONS, FINELY CHOPPED
4 CARROTS, DICED
2 CELERY STICKS, DICED
1 SMALL SWEDE, DICED
2 X 400G CANS GOOD QUALITY
   CHOPPED TOMATOES
SALT AND PEPPER
SPRIG OF ROSEMARY
2 BAY LEAVES
1 BOTTLE DRY WHITE WINE
1.5KG (3LB 5OZ) MARIS PIPER POTATOES,
   PEELED AND QUARTERED
250G (8OZ) SALTED WELSH BUTTER

brecon mutton shepherd's pie

If you've only ever had shepherd's pie made with lamb, you're in for a treat.

Preheat the oven to 140°C/275°F/gas mark 1. Heat a little oil in a flameproof casserole dish and brown the mutton in batches, then set the meat aside. Add a little oil in the casserole dish and brown the onion, carrots, celery and swede together until soft. Add the mutton to the vegetables and mix well before adding the tomatoes, seasoning, rosemary, bay leaves and finally the wine. Bring this to a simmer and transfer to the oven for around 4 hours. The mutton should become very tender.

Cook the potatoes in salted water until tender then mash with the butter. Season well. When the mutton is cooked, skim off the excess fat from the top. Spoon the mutton mixture into one big pie dish, or smaller individual ones, and top with the mash. Turn the oven up to 180°C/350°F/gas mark 4 and then brown the pie or pies the oven for 15–20 minutes.

serves 4

4 × 225G (8OZ) FILLETS OF WELSH BLACK BEEF,
SEASONED WITH FRESHLY GROUND BLACK
PEPPER AND BRUSHED WITH OLIVE OIL

FOR THE HORSERADISH BUTTER

115G (4OZ) SALTED WELSH BUTTER, SOFTENED
1TBSP GOOD QUALITY HORSERADISH SAUCE
1TBSP CHOPPED CHIVES
BLACK PEPPER

FOR THE HERB-STUFFED TOMATOES

55G (2OZ) WHITE BREADCRUMBS
1TBSP ROUGHLY CHOPPED FLAT LEAF PARLEY
1TBSP OLIVE OIL
SALT AND PEPPER
4 VINE-RIPENED TOMATOES

fillet of beef with horseradish butter & baked tomatoes

'Like much else, the success of this simple combination depends on the quality of the raw materials,' say Y Polyn's Susan and Maryann. 'Welsh Black beef is excellent, but it will vary according to how the animal has been kept and how the butcher has looked after the meat. If you can get dry-aged beef (not, as is usual, aged in a plastic shroud) then all the better.'

To make the horseradish butter, place the butter, horseradish sauce and chives in a small blender or food processor and blend until smooth. Grind in a little black pepper and mix again, briefly. Spoon the mixture onto nonstick baking paper and shape into a roll. Refrigerate until it is firm enough to slice.

Preheat the oven to 200°C/400°F/gas mark 6. To prepare the tomatoes, combine the breadcrumbs, parsley and oil and season to taste. Slice tomatoes in half and cut a cross in each half. Top with the crumb mixture. Bake the tomatoes for 10–15 minutes, or until completely tender and slightly golden.

Meanwhile, fry the steaks on both sides in a heavy-based frying pan until cooked to your liking. Leave to rest for a couple of minutes off the heat and season with sea salt. Take 1cm (½ inch) slices of the horseradish butter and place one on top of each steak and allow to melt. Serve with the baked tomatoes. Dauphinoise potatoes and a green salad are good on the side.

makes 3 loaves

750G (1LB 10OZ) SOURDOUGH STARTER (*SEE* OPPOSITE)

500ML (18FL OZ) TEPID WATER

500G (1LB 2OZ) STRONG PLAIN WHITE FLOUR

500G (1LB 2OZ) UNBLEACHED ORGANIC STONEGROUND FLOUR (AT Y POLYN
  WE USE FLOUR FROM BACHELDRE MILL IN MONTGOMERYSHIRE)

3½TSP FINE SEA SALT

SEMOLINA, FOR DUSTING

sourdough bread

Mark's sourdough is second to none and his explanation of how to make
it got me baking my own. I love the way Mark explains how to do it – as
if he is just standing at your shoulder – so I have left it entirely in his own
inimitable voice. Happy baking.

Mark writes: I bake solely by hand because I love the feeling of actually working the dough rather than relying on a food mixer to develop the all-important gluten network. The recipe takes a while to complete. I start it off at about 9am and the loaves are ready to go into the oven at 6pm, but the individual steps are both simple and short. It's easy to make a starter and keep it going. Our starter has been alive for just over two years and, provided you remember to feed it, it's pretty tolerant of occasional neglect.

Weigh out the starter into a big bowl and whisk in the tepid water. Weigh the two flours and measure out the salt, and add all three to the water and starter mix. Bring together the mixture till it forms a soft dough. Cover with a wet tea towel and leave for about an hour in a warm place until the flour has become thoroughly hydrated.

Now the kneading. You don't need to spend ages on this: 30 seconds to a minute's worth of stretching and folding is quite sufficient. You should see at this stage that the dough becomes smoother and much more elastic. Cover the bowl with your wet tea towel again and tuck it back in its cosy corner for another hour to relax and start fermenting.

When you come back you should see that the dough has increased in volume and is beginning to develop some bubbles of gas. Knead the dough for another minute or so and tuck the covered bowl back in its warm place for another hour or so. Then one more round of kneading and resting and you will be ready to shape your loaves.

Divide your dough into six equal portions and give each a final kneading, shaping each piece firstly into a tight ball and then into a neat rugby ball shape. Sourdough is much wetter than yeast-leavened dough and needs some support to hold its shape while it proves. I prove the bread in oval woven breadbaskets lined with napkins liberally sprinkled with semolina. Leave the shaped loaves to prove in their baskets for 3-4 hours, depending on the ambient temperature.

Once the loaves have doubled in size, turn them out on to an oiled and semolina-dusted baking sheet. Slash the tops 4–5 times and bake in a hot oven preheated to 200°C/400°F/gas mark 6 for about 45 minutes, until the crust has developed and the loaves sound hollow when tapped.

SOURDOUGH STARTER

Day 1: Mix 100g (3½oz) white flour, 100g (3½oz) rye flour, 6 raisins, 50g (1¾oz) natural bio yogurt and 150ml (¼ pint) tepid water in a kilner jar and stick it in your airing cupboard or a warm place overnight. **Day 2**: Do nothing. **Day 3**: Chuck away half the mix and refresh the goo that's left with 150g (5½oz) flour and 150ml (¼ pint) water. **Day 4**: You should be seeing some life in the monster now. There should be lots of bubbles of gas and the volume should have increased. Chuck away half the mixture again and make sure all the raisins are gone. This time add 200g (7oz) flour and 150ml (¼ pint) water. **Day 5**: Baking Day. Away you go as per the recipe.

Serves 8

FOR THE SWEET PASTRY

115G (4OZ) UNSALTED BUTTER

85G (3OZ) CASTER SUGAR

PINCH OF SALT

1 EGG YOLK

225G (7½OZ) PLAIN FLOUR

FOR THE FILLING

115G (4OZ) UNSALTED BUTTER

115G (4OZ) CASTER SUGAR

2 EGGS

115G (4OZ) GROUND ALMONDS

4 RIPE PEARS

1 TBSP FLAKED ALMONDS

pear & almond tart

A classic French fruit and frangipane tart. Don't be alarmed at the small amount of frangipane that you spread on the base – it doesn't look like much but it puffs up. The same recipe can be adapted for peaches, nectarines, plums and apricots.

First make the pastry. Whizz the butter in a food processor until soft. Add the sugar and salt and blend further until pale and smooth. Add the egg yolk and then finally add the flour. Blend again. If the mix seems too dry, add a little water. The pastry should come together into a ball. Cover in clingfilm and put in the fridge to rest for a couple of hours.

Roll the pastry out on a lightly floured surface to fit a 28cm/11 inch shallow tart tin with a removable base. Lightly butter the inside of the tart tin and line with the pastry. Put back into the fridge – or the freezer – to chill again. Preheat the oven to 180°C/350°F/gas mark 4.

Bake the tart case blind – line it with nonstick baking paper and baking beans – for 10 minutes. Remove the paper and the beans and cook for a further 5 minutes until lightly coloured and firm. Remove from the oven (but do not turn the oven off) and allow to cool. Cream the butter and sugar for the filling in a food processor until well mixed, then blend in the eggs and then the ground almonds. Pour the mixture into the pastry case and smooth the surface.

Peel the pears and cut into halves. Core the pears then slice them lengthways and fan out. Arrange these on top of the frangipane and sprinkle with flaked almonds. Bake with the oven still at 180°C/350°F/gas mark 4 for 30–40 minutes. The surface should be golden and just set and the pears should be tender. At Y Polyn this is served with Pembrokeshire clotted cream or good vanilla ice cream.

'Everything is fitting, from the slate tablemats to the no-nonsense farmhouse-style napkins, the homemade piccalilli to the Welsh cheeses. "We like the ordinary done very well", says Mark. And that is exactly what they do here. Superlatively.'

the best of the rest

the angel

The exterior of The Angel suggests a cared for, well-run place and the bar here is indeed a big draw – full of well-worn comfy sofas, mirrors and twinkling lights. It has a lovely, slightly eccentric vibe and the staff are salt of the earth. Food, from former Welsh chef of the year, Rod Peterson, spans gastropub and brasserie classics: kedgeree with poached egg, terrines with homemade chutney and duck confit. It's spot on.

Salem, Llandeilo, Carmarthenshire, SA19 7LY Tel. 01558 823394, www.angelsalem.co.uk Serves lunch (except Sunday, Monday and Tuesday) and dinner (except Sunday and Monday).

the harbourmaster hotel

Owners Glyn and Menna Heulyn have turned The Harbourmaster, an old whaling inn, into a chic but unpretentious small hotel with a great bar and a superb dining room. The outside is a stunning cobalt blue while inside it's all chunky tables and contemporary fabrics. Dishes show off the best local produce and are extremely well done. The location – right on the harbour – is unsurpassable. Fishing boats come and go by day and lights twinkle on the water at night. The place is so 'in' that it's been featured in *Grazia* as a celeb hangout, but don't let that put you off.

Pen Cei, Aberaeron, Ceredigion, SA46 0BA Tel. 01545 570755, www.harbour-master.com. Serves lunch (except Monday) and dinner (except Sunday), rooms available.

the kinmel arms

A pub and restaurant with stunning bedrooms not far from Snowdonia, this place is smart. The inside is full of light, wooden floors and neutral colours, and there's a big conservatory restaurant as well as a splendid bar. Food is unfussy and very well executed. You might find a tart of Perl Lâs cheese, Welsh rib-eye steak, or cod with homemade tartare sauce. Cask ales are one of the owners' passions, and there's a good wine list too. It's a great place for a weekend break – the bedrooms are simply stunning.

The Village, St George, Abergele, Conwy, LL22 9BP Tel. 01745 832207, www.thekinmelarms.co.uk. Serves lunch (except Monday) and dinner (except Sunday), rooms available.

the stables bar restaurant

A stunning-looking place. The old stable of Soughton Hall has been turned into a stylish country space of cobbled floors, bare brick, chunky beams and high ceilings. Perch on old metal bar stools while you drink beers from local breweries or eat simple dishes, such as shepherd's pie, beef burgers and sausages with mash, based on local produce. The food is good rather than amazing – it's the space and the drink that score here. There is no wine list – diners can browse and buy in the adjoining wine shop, which specializes in South African wines. All this plus a gorgeous outdoor dining area, with wooden furniture and pebbles underfoot, in a setting of glorious parkland.

Soughton Hall, Northop, Mold, Flintshire, CH7 6AB Tel. 01352 840577, www.soughtonhall.co.uk. Serves lunch and dinner every day, rooms available in Soughton Hall.

bunch of grapes

What a find! A gorgeous little place – smart and modern – but still a pub. Furnished with solid tables and fresh flowers, and tealights twinkling in the evening. The food is modern but also feels Welsh – Caws-y-Craig bread, potted Penclawdd cockles, beer-battered pollack and local lamb with salsa verde. The kitchen cares – only sustainable fish is used and most of the produce is local – and there's a terrific range of real ales and ciders.

Ynysangharad Road, Pontypridd, Glamorgan, CF3 4DA Tel. 01443 402934, www.bunchofgrapes.org.uk

the raglan arms

The village local – it can get very busy – as well as a decent pit-stop, The Raglan Arms is much smarter than you might expect from the outside – leather sofas, slate floor, a space filled with light. There are some great sandwiches – roast Gloucester Old Spot pork with chunky apple sauce on home-baked bread, for example – and both simple and cosmopolitan main courses such as the Turkish aubergine dish, imam bayaldi, or salmon with a tomato salsa. There's an interesting wine list, as well as local ales.

Llandenny, Usk, Monmouthshire, NP15 1DL Tel. 01291 690800, www.raglanarms.com. Serves lunch (except Monday) and dinner (except Sunday and Monday).

the northwest

Chef Nigel Haworth is a bit of a legend in these parts. He has a Michelin-starred gaff down the road – Northcote Manor – and his energy is astounding: running cookery classes, arranging trips for visiting chefs, giving lectures. His greatest achievement (and it was never an aim, more something Nigel just did naturally) has been the championing of local produce, backing the farmers who work around him and singing the praises of regionality. He has been using the current buzz-words of 'local' and 'regional' for a quarter of a century now, and way before they became fashionable.

It is fitting that he now runs not one but two pubs serving regional food (the other is The Highwayman in the guide section, and he has another due to open shortly). 'I love to do something new. I like a challenge. So that was part of the reason I decided to open a pub,' says Nigel. 'But I also just love pubs. To me they mean flagstone floors, bare wood, real ales, open fires and the kind of food your mum makes. It also seemed like a good place to showcase food made by local producers more simply. I'm really proud of our cheese board, for example.' Another spur was the democratization of eating out. 'I think everybody should be able to eat really good food and I wasn't reaching that many people through fine dining,' he says.

The Three Fishes certainly does feed a lot of folk. It's a big, solid-looking building right beside the road with a sprawling network of rooms, a handsome bar and acres of wood and flagstones. The only drawback to the place is its size, which rather mitigates against cosiness. Get there early and grab a table near one of the fires.

Nigel's suppliers look down at you from the black-and-white photographs on the wall and even adorn the table mats. There's a useful foodie map of who's who in the area on the back of the hunger-inducing menu. As for the dishes, you want to eat everything: chips cooked in dripping, local mutton with red cabbage, Andrew Ireland's black pudding with onion relish or the 'Length of Lancashire' cheese board (10 local cheeses of different ages). And localness is taken very seriously. The Lancashire hotpot – a must – is made with heather-reared Bowland lamb at The Three Fishes, but Cumbrian fell-bred lamb at The Highwayman, even though the two are only 40 miles apart.

It's great that this part of England has such places to show off its wonderful cheeses, poultry and lamb to a wide audience, and there has been a mini explosion of good dining pubs in Lancashire since Nigel opened The Three Fishes. Once again he is blazing a trail.

the three fishes

MITTON ROAD, MITTON, NEAR WHALLEY, LANCASHIRE, BB7 9PQ • TEL 01254 826888 • www.thethreefishes.com
SERVES LUNCH AND DINNER EVERY DAY

Serves 2

FOR THE FILLING

80G (3OZ) ONION, FINELY CHOPPED

50ML (2FL OZ) WATER

10G (¼OZ) BUTTER

SALT AND WHITE PEPPER

150G (7OZ) ORGANIC CREAMY LANCASHIRE
  CHEESE, GRATED

50G (1¾OZ) CURD CHEESE

FOR THE PASTRY

200G (7OZ) PLAIN FLOUR

PINCH OF SALT

100G (3½OZ) BUTTER, DICED, NOT FRIDGE-COLD

3 EGG YOLKS, PLUS 1 EGG, BEATEN, TO GLAZE

WATER, TO BIND

leagram's organic creamy lancashire cheese & onion pie

Sounds ordinary but is divine...

To make the filling, place the onion, water and butter in a pan. Bring to the boil then season with salt and pepper. Allow to cook until just tender then remove from the heat, cool and drain off the liquid. Mix the two cheeses together.

To make the pastry, sieve the flour into a bowl with the salt. Add the butter and rub into the flour until the mixture resembles breadcrumbs. Make a well in the centre, add the yolk and a little water and mix together until a smooth dough is formed. Cover in clingfilm and leave to rest for about 2 hours in the fridge.

Preheat the oven to 180°C/350°F/gas mark 4. On a lightly floured surface, roll out the pastry to approximately 2mm (⅛ inch) thick. Cut out 2 circles to fit an 18cm (7 inch) enamel pie tin, with one circle just slightly larger than the other. Line the base of the tin with the smaller circle of pastry and fill with alternate layers of cheese and the onion mix until the pie is full. Cover with the pastry lid, pressing down to crimp the edges, and brush with beaten egg to glaze. Bake for 15–20 minutes or until golden. Serve with a baked potato and a tomato salad.

Serves 4

100G (3½OZ) BUTTER

500G (1LB 2OZ) SLICED ONIONS

2½TSP SALT

1.2KG (2LB 12OZ) DICED
  STEWING LAMB

1TSP SUGAR

PINCH OF WHITE PEPPER

2TSP PLAIN FLOUR

300ML (10FL OZ) CHICKEN STOCK

1KG (2LB 4OZ) POTATOES (MARIS
  PIPER OR WILJA), PEELED AND
  THINLY SLICED

FOR THE RED CABBAGE (12 PORTIONS)

1 RED CABBAGE

55G (2OZ) COARSE SEA SALT

275ML (9½FL OZ) MALT VINEGAR

140ML (5FL OZ) WHITE WINE VINEGAR

140ML (5FL OZ) BALSAMIC VINEGAR

400ML (14FL OZ) RED WINE

300G (10½OZ) CASTER SUGAR

2 STAR ANISE

5 BAY LEAVES

10 CLOVES

1TSP BLACK PEPPERCORNS

1TSP PINK PEPPERCORNS

1 CINNAMON STICK

5 WHOLE DRIED RED CHILLIES

20 JUNIPER BERRIES

heather-reared bowland lamb lancashire hotpot with pickled red cabbage

Nigel uses the fattier cuts, from the forequarter (neck and shoulder), for this hotpot, which is famed throughout Lancashire, and beyond.

Preheat the oven to 160°C/325°F/gas mark 3. Melt one-quarter of the butter in a heavy-based pan and sweat the onions over a medium heat until soft. Add 1 tsp salt then sweat for a few minutes more. Season the meat with the remaining salt, the sugar and some pepper and dust with flour. Place in a deep casserole with a third of the stock, then put the onions on top of the meat. Put a sheet of greaseproof paper on the meat, cover with a lid or tin foil, and bake for 2 hours. Remove and allow to cool. Preheat the oven to 200°C/400°F/gas mark 6.

Put the rest of the chicken stock and the butter in a saucepan and bring to the boil. Blanch the potatoes quickly for 1 minute, then drain well. Remove and allow to cool.

Divide the cooked lamb between 4 hotpot dishes (or one larger one). Place the onions on top, then a neat layer of potatoes. Melt the remaining butter and brush over the potatoes. Bake for 30 minutes and serve with a spoonful of the pickled red cabbage.

To make the cabbage, finely slice it, discarding the tough central core. Salt well in a colander and leave for 2 hours. Wash, drain well and pat dry. Put the vinegars, wine and sugar in a pan, bring to the boil and reduce by half. Place all the dry ingredients in a pestle and mortar and pound to get a coarse mixture, then add to the reduction and infuse for 5 minutes. Pass through a fine sieve and, while still hot, pour onto the red cabbage in 2 x 1.5 litre (2½ pints) sterilized Kilner jars. Put the lids on, allow to cool and refrigerate until needed (it is best after a couple of weeks).

'Pubs to me mean flagstone floors, bare wood, real ales, open fires and the kind of food your mum makes. A pub is also a good place to showcase food made by local producers.'

Serves 4

FOR THE MONKFISH
4 MONKFISH TAILS, SKINNED
   AND TRIMMED
PLAIN FLOUR
1 EGG YOLK
JAPANESE BREADCRUMBS,
   FOR COATING
OIL FOR DEEP-FRYING

FOR THE MAYONNAISE
3 EGG YOLKS
1TSP ENGLISH MUSTARD
1TSP WHITE WINE VINEGAR
LEMON JUICE, TO TASTE

SALT AND PEPPER
150ML (5FL OZ) SUNFLOWER OIL
1TBSP EXTRA VIRGIN OLIVE OIL
100G (3½OZ) PICKLED ONIONS, CHOPPED
20G (¾OZ) VERY SMALL CAPERS
20G (¾OZ) FINELY SLICED GHERKINS
2TBSP CHOPPED FLAT LEAF PARSLEY

FOR THE PEA PURÉE
600G (1LB 5OZ) FROZEN PEAS, DEFROSTED
200G (7OZ) BUTTER
SALT AND PEPPER
2 PINCHES CASTER SUGAR
50ML (2FL OZ) CHICKEN STOCK

deep-fried monkfish tail in breadcrumbs with garden pea purée and caper & onion mayonnaise

Fish and chips gone posh. The pea purée is delicious, even if you're not a mushy pea fan.

First make the mayonnaise. Mix the egg yolks, mustard, white wine vinegar, lemon juice and salt and pepper together in a food processor. With the motor running slowly, add the oils a little at a time, beating well after each addition, until the mixture thickens. Season to taste. Add all the other ingredients, mix together and taste again for seasoning. Keep in the fridge, covered, until you need it.

Place half the defrosted peas in a pan with the butter, salt, pepper, sugar and chicken stock and cook until the peas are soft. Place in a liquidizer and blend until you get a smooth purée. Boil the rest of the peas for 1 minute and fold into the purée.

Dust the monkfish tails in flour then dip them in egg yolk, then the Japanese breadcrumbs. Deep-fry for 4 minutes in oil heated to 180°C/350°F. The crust should be a lovely golden colour.

Place some pea purée in the middle of a large plate and put a deep-fried monkfish tail on top. Put a dollop of mayonnaise to one side and serve with chunky chips.

1 pie serves 2 people

150G (5½OZ) BUTTER

300G (10½OZ) PLAIN FLOUR

50G (1¾OZ) CASTER SUGAR

GRATED RIND OF ½ LEMON

1 MEDIUM EGG, BEATEN

A LITTLE EGG YOLK, TO SEAL PASTRY

50ML (2FL OZ) MILK

FOR THE APPLE FILLING

400G (14OZ) BRAMLEY APPLES

50G (1¾OZ) CASTER SUGAR, PLUS EXTRA
  FOR DUSTING

TO SERVE

1 SMALL TIN CARNATION MILK

A WEDGE OF MRS KIRKHAM'S
  LANCASHIRE CHEESE

bramley apple pie, carnation milk & mrs kirkham's lancashire cheese

The portions at The Three Fishes are pretty big but you should just rest for an hour after your main course, drink a bit more, and then order this. This is the best kind of comfort food, and a real treat to get it with Carnation milk (as if you were at your granny's). Do try to find Mrs Kirkham's Lancashire cheese to go alongside it.

Rub the butter, flour, sugar and lemon rind together with your fingers until the mixture resembles breadcrumbs. Add the beaten egg a little at a time, until the pastry comes together. Wrap in clingfilm and chill for 20–30 minutes.

To make the filling, peel, core and slice the apples. Put in a small saucepan and add the sugar. Cook on the stove until just tender, or slightly undercooked. Allow to cool.

Preheat the oven to 170°C/325°F/gas mark 3. Roll out the pastry and cut into two discs about 2mm (⅛th inch) thick, using an 18cm (7inch) enamel pie dish to mark out your circles and making one slightly bigger than the other. Line the pie dish with the smaller pastry disc, and put the cooked apples in the centre of the pie dish. Brush the pastry edge with a little egg. Place the other pastry disc on top and gently press down, crimping the two edges together to make a perfect seal. With a small, sharp knife, make two little slits in the centre. Brush with a little milk and sprinkle with caster sugar. Bake for 15–20 minutes, or until golden brown.

On a wooden board, place a jug of Carnation milk. Then place the enamel pie dish on the centre and serve with a wedge of Mrs Kirkham's Lancashire cheese.

serves 4

FOR THE DRESSING
100ML (3½FL OZ) WORCESTERSHIRE SAUCE
50ML (2FL OZ) APPLE JUICE

FOR THE CHEESE ON TOAST
4 SLICES ORGANIC WHITE BREAD
8 RASHERS GOOD QUALITY DRY-CURED STREAKY BACON
KNOB OF BUTTER
200G (7OZ) LANCASHIRE CHEESE (THE THREE FISHES USES SHORROCKS), SLICED

lancashire cheese on toast with bacon & worcester sauce dressing

There are some great dishes on the menu at The Three Fishes but this is my favourite, and anyone can cook it. Cheese on toast doesn't come any better.

To make the dressing, boil the Worcestershire sauce and the apple juice together and reduce by half until it is quite syrupy.

Preheat the grill. Toast the bread on each side and cook the bacon till crispy. Butter the toast on both sides and cover one side with Lancashire cheese. Place on a baking sheet, then grill until the cheese has melted. Place the cheese on toast on warm plates, put the bacon on top and drizzle with the dressing.

the best of the rest

the punch bowl inn

The Punch Bowl was in my previous book on gastropubs but it has since changed hands and undergone a complete refurbishment so earns a new entry here. The owners of the beautifully designed Drunken Duck in Barngates bought the place and have done a gorgeous job. The long bar has a slate top, there are flowers on all the tables and flagstones on the floor, and the dining room is smarter than of old, with gleaming wooden floorboards, white tablecloths and chic leather chairs. The place does still manage to be a pub, despite the new design, and plenty of people drop in for a pint and a ploughman's. Food-wise, it doesn't reach the heights scaled by the pub's previous incumbent, Steven Doherty, but the cooking is good nonetheless and sourcing is local: Morecambe Bay shrimps with salad leaves, lamb in many guises, braises using the inn's own brew – Tag Lag – and good fish dishes.
Crosthwaite, Lyth Valley, Cumbria, LA8 8HR
Tel. 01539 568237, www.the-punchbowl.co.uk
Serves lunch and dinner every day, rooms available.

bay horse inn

Great pubby atmosphere – open fires and real ales – and you can eat in the bar or the dining room. Most of the dishes sound down-to-earth but chef Craig Wilkinson is an ambitious and talented cook, and dishes are less ordinary than they read. Food is local, from the Forest of Bowland and the Lakes. Farmer Reg Johnson's famous Goosnargh duck is slow-cooked with prunes and the Lancashire hotpot is made with Cumbrian mutton and served with pickled red cabbage. Fish pie is topped with a glorious cheesy mash and the sticky toffee pudding is about as gooey as it comes.
Bay Horse Lane, Forton, Lancashire, LA2 0HR
Tel. 01524 791204, www.bayhorseinn.com. Serves lunch
(except Monday) and dinner (except Sunday and Monday).

the freemason's arms

On weekend evenings all roads around here seem to lead to this glowing little pub down a tiny alley in the small village of Wiswell, and there's quite a queue of taxis dropping off and collecting. It's not surprising that people don't take chances with driving themselves – you will definitely drink too much as the wine list is superb. You'll spend a long time craning your neck to read the list of bin ends above the bar, as well as going through the two tomes of lists (one for everyday bottles, the other for special ones, some of which will hit your wallet hard) before choosing. Specials are on a board and there's a printed menu too. There's crispy pork belly with lentils, tempura of sea bass with garlic mayo, and duck confit, and more traditional pubby food such as steaks and fish pie. Drinkers are welcome at the bar, and if they don't fancy the wine they can down a pint of ale. And then order a cab.
8 Vicarage Fold, Wiswell, Lancashire, BB7 9DF
Tel. 01254 822218, www.freemasonswiswell.co.uk
Serves lunch (except Monday and Tuesday) and
dinner (except Monday, Tuesday and Sunday).

the highwayman

Another pub run by Nigel Haworth and his pub group, Ribble Valley Inns, who own The Three Fishes at Mitton. The Highwayman has much the same feel design-wise – big chunky flagstones and warm solid furniture – and many of the dishes are similar, but Nigel does try to keep some offerings special to The Highwayman. He always manages to offer the traditional with just that little bit extra: potted wild boar (from local farmer, Peter Gott) with pork dripping on toast, Herdwick mutton shepherd's pie with creamed onions and capers, or suckling pig with honeyed white cabbage and spring onion mash. It makes you feel good just to read the names of such dishes.
Burrow, Lancashire, LA6 2RJ, Tel. 01524 273338
www.highwaymaninn.co.uk. Serves lunch and dinner.

the inn at whitewell

You're glad to see this place when it appears (and you'll probably get lost trying to find it, though the pub helpfully have a whole section on 'how not to get lost trying to find us' on their website). Everything about it feels right – open fires around every corner, tartan-covered chairs, dark furniture, worn rugs on the floors, old pictures on the walls, and a general air of shabby-genteel grandeur. You can eat in the bar or in the more formal dining room but the bar has the best view of the astounding countryside (it looks right over the River Hodder). Eat black pudding from Bury with mustard mash, homemade baked beans or a cracking fish pie. It all hits the spot.

Whitewell, Lancashire, BB7 3AT
Tel. 01200 448222, www.innatwhitewell.com
Serves lunch and dinner every day, rooms available.

spread eagle

This won't be to everyone's taste – it's all swirly carpets and old-fashioned dark pub furniture (it certainly predates the gastropub look) – but the food in the bar, a shorter version of the à la carte available in the dining room, is very good value and there's a great range of wines and whiskies. The dining room is in a 1970s extension and has the feel of a provincial hotel, but nevertheless possesses a kind of retro charm. The wild mushroom risotto is one of the best I've ever tasted and is made with a great, rich stock. Chef Greig Barnes does a mean gravlax as well, here served with beetroot, and a bread-and-butter pudding, served with apricot compote, to die for. The dining room looks over the lovely River Ribble, which would cheer even the hardest of hearts.

Sawley, Lancashire, BB7 4NH, Tel. 01200 441202
www.the-spreadeagle.co.uk. Serves lunch (except Monday) and dinner (except Sunday and Monday).

white bull

A remarkably handsome pub in the middle of this small village, The White Bull dates from the early 1700s and does indeed have a wooden white bull (a strange art naïf construction) hanging outside. Inside, it is very much a regular old-fashioned pub kitted out in the way brewery-owned pubs are – dark green carpet, non-descript chunky dark furniture and green table mats. The young leaseholders, Christopher and Kath Bell don't have enough money to make much of a difference, though they've done their best with glowing lamps and antique ephemera. Chris won a Gordon Ramsay scholarship and worked for him at Claridges before heading north to Preston to work at Paul Heathcote's restaurant, Longridge. The dishes are solid – Bury black pudding fritters, slow-cooked shank of Cumbrian fell-bred lamb, smoked haddock and leek bake with Mrs Kirkham's Lancashire cheese mash – but very well done and just what you want in a pub.

Water Street, Ribchester, Lancashire, PR3 3XP
Tel. 01254 878303, www.whitebullrib.co.uk
Serves lunch (except Monday) and dinner (except Monday and just early supper on Sunday), rooms available.

yorkshire and the
northeast

You wouldn't go to The Fox and Hounds if you weren't in the know. Stuck on a promontory overlooking the sea in a little-known village in Yorkshire, it looks like a farm outbuilding and not a place where you would expect to have a gastronomic experience. Which is why it's all the more wonderful when you do. Certainly the atmosphere among the diners – many of them locals who come frequently – is one of shared glee that this place is so tucked away and so special.

Apart from the food, the main joy is the total lack of design. Owners Sue Wren and Jason Davies (Sue does front of house, Jason cooks and they live upstairs with their children) pulled together whatever they could and furnished the place on a shoestring. There's a trad swirly carpet, a small unrevamped bar, red velvet banquettes, old Singer sewing-machine tables and a couple of stools that wouldn't look out of place in Peter Stringfellow's. It doesn't even make shabby chic but is truly a one-off: a creation that only a tiny budget and serendipity could produce.

As soon as you open the front door you sense the style of the cooking. The small kitchen is right beside the entrance and the sound of pans and the smell of warming olive oil envelop you. Jason does everything himself and the menu reads like you are in some northern outpost of London's River Café, with Italy writ large. Jason never cooked at the River Café (though he did put in time at The Ivy in London) but his food is as good as you'll get in the eateries well-travelled foodies swoon over. It's the sort of no-nonsense cooking that depends on prime ingredients and careful handling: perfect silky ravioli of pumpkin with brown sage butter; lamb's kidneys with Puy lentils, chilli and garlic; sweet monkfish fillet wrapped in prosciutto with pea, potato and broad bean braise; juicy chicken-liver crostini with anchovy and capers – you just want to move into the village for a week and come here for lunch every day.

The dishes may be Italian but as many ingredients as possible come from Yorkshire and locally caught fish is a dominant feature. When it comes to the cheese course we are firmly in God's own counties – there's no taleggio or fontina but farmhouse cheeses from Yorkshire and Lancashire. And did I mention the puddings? They offer the likes of rustic pears cooked in red wine and a dark, properly grown-up chocolate truffle cake that could probably kill you (but what a sweet death…).

All of this is delivered, as you might expect from the surroundings, without any folderol or fanfares on inexpensive white plates and with modest charm. The wine list is sound and strong on Italians and there are no less than eight pudding wines (oh joy!) to round off your meal. Little wonder the locals who pack the place out look so pleased with themselves…

the fox and hounds

GOLDSBOROUGH, WHITBY, NORTH YORKSHIRE, YO21 3RX • TEL 01947 893372
SERVES LUNCH (WED–SUN) AND DINNER (WED–SAT)

serves 4

4 x 200G (7OZ) CHUNKY PIECES OF
   HALIBUT FILLET, WITH SKIN
SEA SALT AND BLACK PEPPER
EXTRA VIRGIN OLIVE OIL
400G (14OZ) SPINACH

FOR THE LEMON OIL
JUICE OF 1 LEMON
EXTRA VIRGIN OLIVE OIL

FOR THE PORCINI POTATOES
100G (3½OZ) DRIED PORCINI
   MUSHROOMS
1KG (2LB 4OZ) CHARLOTTE OR
   SIMILAR WAXY POTATOES
1TBSP EXTRA VIRGIN OLIVE OIL
100G (3½OZ) UNSALTED BUTTER
SEA SALT AND BLACK PEPPER
1TBSP FRESH THYME LEAVES

seared halibut fillet with baked porcini potatoes, spinach and lemon oil

Jason has a lot of very simple fish dishes in his repertoire and makes the best of the local catch, even though he gives it an Italian, rather than a Yorkshire, treatment.

Preheat the oven to 200°C/400°F/gas mark 6.

To make the lemon oil, mix the lemon juice with three times the amount of extra virgin olive oil.

For the potatoes, soak the porcini in 650ml (1 pint 2fl oz) boiling water for 15 minutes then strain through a sieve, keeping the soaking water. Rinse the porcini under cold running water to remove any grit, then dry them.

Cut the potatoes in half lengthways. Heat the olive oil with the butter in a roasting tin and, when the butter is foaming, add the porcini. Cook and stir for a minute before adding the porcini liquor. Bring to the boil and add the potatoes. Season with salt, pepper and thyme. Cover with tin foil and place in the oven. After 15 minutes, turn the potatoes over and continue baking for a further 15 minutes, or until soft, and keep warm. Do not turn the oven off.

Season the halibut fillets with salt and pepper. Heat an ovenproof frying pan and add a couple of tablespoons of olive oil. When smoking, place the halibut fillets in, skin-side down, and cook for 1 minute, then transfer to the oven and continue to cook (still skin-side down) until the flesh side of the halibut has changed from an opaque to a white colour. Remove from the oven and set aside.

Heat another pan, add a couple of tablespoons of olive oil and the spinach and wilt the spinach. Season. Remove from the heat. When you're ready to serve, turn the halibut fillets over, divide the porcini potatoes and the spinach between 4 plates, put the halibut skin-side up on top and spoon some of the lemon oil around.

'The atmosphere among the diners –
many of them locals who come
frequently – is one of shared glee
that this place is so tucked away.'

serves 4

400G (14OZ) OAK-ROAST SALMON

300G (10½OZ) FLOURY
  POTATOES, PEELED

SEMOLINA FLOUR

OLIVE OIL

400G (14OZ) SPINACH, WASHED AND
  ANY COARSE STALKS REMOVED

4TBSP EXTRA VIRGIN OLIVE OIL

SALT AND PEPPER

FOR THE PARSLEY SAUCE

500ML (18FL OZ) MILK

COUPLE OF SLICES OF ONION

1 BAY LEAF

A FEW PARSLEY STALKS

40G (1½OZ) UNSALTED BUTTER

40G (1½OZ) PLAIN FLOUR

SEA SALT AND PEPPER

FRESHLY GRATED NUTMEG

2TBSP CHOPPED FLAT LEAF PARSLEY

oak-roast salmon fishcake with spinach & parsley sauce

Fishcakes are legion in dining pubs, but these, made with hot smoked salmon, are just a little bit different.

To make the fishcakes, flake the smoked salmon. Boil the potatoes in salted water until tender. Drain really well and mash. Allow the potato to cool, then add the smoked salmon and season with salt and pepper. Mix to combine. Shape into 4 patties and dust with semolina flour. Chill in the fridge for 45 minutes or so.

For the parsley sauce, put the milk, onion, bay leaf and parsley stalks in a heavy-based saucepan and heat until just below boiling. Remove from the heat and leave to infuse for 10 minutes. Strain the milk into a jug, clean the pan and melt the butter in it. Add the flour and stir well, then cook gently for 2 minutes until you have a straw-coloured mixture. Take the pan off the heat and gradually add the warm milk, whisking constantly. Put the pan back on the heat and bring to the boil, stirring constantly. The mixture will thicken considerably. Reduce the heat and simmer for 10 minutes, whisking frequently. Season with salt, pepper and nutmeg, to taste, and add the chopped parsley. Set aside and keep warm.

Preheat the oven to 220°C/425°F/gas mark 7. Heat an ovenproof frying pan, add some olive oil, then the fishcakes and cook over a high heat for a minute or so until golden on each side. Transfer to the oven and cook for 5 minutes, then turn them over and cook for a further 5 minutes. Wilt the spinach in another pan with the extra virgin olive oil. Season well.

To serve, divide the spinach between 4 plates, put a fishcake on top and spoon some parsley sauce on top of the fishcake.

serves 6

½ PORK BELLY, SKIN SCORED
  (ABOUT 1KG/2LB 4OZ)
EXTRA VIRGIN OLIVE OIL
SEA SALT
600G (1LB 5OZ) RAINBOW CHARD

FOR THE BEANS
2TSP BICARBONATE OF SODA
200G (7OZ) DRIED CANNELLINI BEANS

½ HEAD GARLIC
JUICE OF 1 LEMON
6TBSP EXTRA VIRGIN OLIVE OIL
SEA SALT AND BLACK PEPPER

slow roast pork belly with cannellini beans

Jason advises that you make this dish over the course of two days as it's in two stages. The first stage involves cooking the pork belly and soaking the beans in a generous amount of cold water with the bicarbonate of soda. This can be done overnight. The next day is the cooking and serving.

Preheat the oven to 140°C/275°F/gas mark 1. Rub the skin side of the pork belly with olive oil and sea salt and place in a roasting tin. Add a cup of water and place in the oven, then leave to cook overnight or for 10 hours. Dissolve the bicarbonate of soda in a bowl of water and soak the beans in the solution for 10 hours or overnight.

Remove the pork from the oven and place on a tray. Allow to cool, then put in the fridge for a couple of hours to firm up. Add some more water to the roasting tin that held the pork, place on a high heat and scrape to create a thin sauce. Put the juice through a sieve into a jug and reserve. Once the fat has settled on the top skim it off and discard. Drain the beans, place in a saucepan, cover with cold water, bring to the boil and simmer for 10 minutes. Drain again and pour in fresh cold water to cover by about 5cm (2inches). Add the garlic. Return to the boil and simmer, removing any scum that comes to the surface, for about 1–1½ hours, or until the beans are cooked.

Preheat the oven to 220°C/425°F/gas mark 7. Remove the pork from the fridge, cut into six pieces, and place in an oven for 15–20 minutes until the skin crackles. Drain the beans and mix with the lemon juice, olive oil, salt and pepper. Prepare the chard by cutting out the tough central stalks and washing the leaves. Wilt the rainbow chard in a pan with some olive oil and season. (You can use the stalks for soup, or chop them up and soften them in the pan with some olive oil before adding the leaves.) Reheat the roasting juices.

To serve, divide the beans and chard between 6 plates, put a piece of pork belly on top and spoon the roasting juices around.

venison & wild boar sausages with lentils & curly kale

Use other spicy Italian sausages – based on pork – if you can't find any made with venison and wild boar.

serves 4

8 FAT VENISON AND WILD BOAR SAUSAGES
400G (14OZ) CURLY KALE, TOUGH CENTRAL
  STALKS REMOVED

FOR THE LENTILS

175G (6OZ) PUY LENTILS
3TBSP EXTRA VIRGIN OLIVE OIL
JUICE OF 1 LEMON
1TSP DIJON MUSTARD
SEA SALT AND BLACK PEPPER

FOR THE MUSTARD DRESSING

1TBSP WHOLEGRAIN MUSTARD
2TBSP WHITE WINE VINEGAR
6TBSP EXTRA VIRGIN OLIVE OIL

Preheat the oven to 220°C/425°F/gas mark 7. To make the mustard dressing, put the mustard in a small bowl with the vinegar and whisk in the olive oil to emulsify. Set aside until needed. Wash the lentils and place in a large saucepan. Cover with plenty of cold water and bring to the boil. Turn the heat down and simmer gently for about 20 minutes or until the lentils are al dente.

While the lentils are cooking, roast the sausages in a roasting tin in the hot oven, turning from time to time until cooked and coloured on all sides (about 15 minutes). Meanwhile, blanch the curly kale in salted boiling water until tender, drain and toss in some of the mustard dressing. Drain the cooked lentils and return to the pan. Toss in the olive oil and lemon juice, stir in the mustard and season. To serve, divide the lentils and kale between 4 plates, put the sausages on top and spoon the rest of the dressing around.

crab linguini with chilli, fennel and lemon

This Italian classic is a cinch if your fishmonger can sell you fresh white crab meat.

serves 4

350G (12OZ) LINGUINI
2TBSP EXTRA VIRGIN OLIVE OIL, PLUS EXTRA
  FOR DRIZZLING
1 CLOVE GARLIC, FINELY CHOPPED
1TBSP CRUSHED FENNEL SEEDS
1 DRIED CHILLI, CRUMBLED
350G (12OZ) WHITE CRAB MEAT
JUICE AND GRATED RIND OF 1 LEMON
SALT AND PEPPER
2TBSP CHOPPED FENNEL LEAVES

Cook the linguini in plenty of salted boiling water until al dente.

Meanwhile, heat the olive oil in a heavy-based pan, add the garlic, fennel seeds and chilli and cook to soften, without colouring. Add the crab, lemon juice and rind and seasoning to taste. Stir as you gently heat the mixture.

When the pasta is ready, drain and add to the crab mixture along with the fennel leaves. Stir to combine – adding a little more olive oil if you want to – and serve.

serves 10

450G (1LB) PLAIN DARK CHOCOLATE (YOU NEED
EXCELLENT STUFF, WITH 70% COCOA SOLIDS)
600ML (1 PINT) DOUBLE CREAM
COCOA POWDER

FOR THE MASCARPONE CREAM
300ML (½ PINT) DOUBLE CREAM
1TBSP ICING SUGAR (OR MORE TO TASTE)
250G (9OZ) MASCARPONE
1 SHOT STRONG ESPRESSO

chocolate truffle cake with espresso mascarpone cream

Yes, this dessert could nearly kill you, but what a way to go…

Break the chocolate into pieces and melt in a bowl set over simmering water. You must not let the chocolate get too hot; the bowl should be in steam, not in water. Warm the cream and stir into the warm chocolate.

Place a 20cm (8inch) cake ring on a flat plate. Pour the mixture into the ring and leave to set for 3 hours in the fridge. To remove the cake from the ring, place a hot dishcloth around the ring to slightly melt the edge of the cake and lift it off. Dust the top of the cake with cocoa powder.

For the mascarpone cream, whisk the cream with the icing sugar until it forms soft peaks. In another bowl, mix the mascarpone with the shot of espresso and incorporate the cream into this mixture. Use a hot knife to cut the cake and serve with the mascarpone cream.

serves 4

2 VANILLA PODS

200G (7OZ) CASTER SUGAR

100G (3½OZ) UNSALTED BUTTER

500G (1LB 2OZ) PLUMS, HALVED AND
STONES REMOVED

4 SLICES SOURDOUGH OR OTHER COARSE COUNTRY
BREAD, APPROX 1CM (½INCH) THICK

JUICE OF 1 LEMON

150G (5FL OZ) CRÈME FRAÎCHE

plum & vanilla bruschetta with crème fraîche

A wonderfully simple dessert, this is great to eat after a laid-back Sunday lunch.

Preheat oven to 180°C/350°F/gas mark 4.

Split the vanilla pods, scrape out the seeds and mix with the sugar. Use some of the butter to grease an ovenproof dish and place the plums in it cut side up. Scatter over half the vanilla sugar. Bake for 15 minutes. Remove the dish from the oven (but do not turn the oven off) and spoon out the plums, leaving the juices in the dish.

Butter the bread, place in the baking dish, buttered-side up, scatter over the rest of the vanilla sugar and pile the plums on top. Squeeze over the lemon juice. Bake for a further 15 minutes. Remove when the bread is crisp at the edges. Serve with the cooking juices and crème fraîche.

The Pipe and Glass Inn is exactly what you want to see at the end of a day's walking (or driving). A sprawling 15th-century hostelry with curls of smoke rising from its many chimneys, it is tucked away at the end of a country road. You're just dying to get beside one of those fires and order a ploughman's. The first thing I saw on entering was, indeed, a ploughman's, or rather armfuls of them: mounds of homemade chutneys and piccalilli with cheeses from Yorkshire and Lancashire, all laid out on gorgeous-looking slate boards.

The owners, James Mackenzie and Kate Burroughs (he cooks, she does front-of-house) have gone down the chic route style-wise, while managing to maintain the place as a pub. The Pipe and Glass is big, with several large dining rooms furnished with leather chesterfields, smart chairs and church pews. The main bar is a bit more traditional but the colour palette is neutral and the materials are natural. The same menu is served throughout. The Pipe and Glass is undoubtedly smart but it's not chintzy or sterile. The place exudes warmth. 'It's funny,' says James. 'Gastropubs are almost synonymous with bareness but we didn't want that – we wanted people to feel they could bury themselves here for an afternoon and get a sense of wellbeing.'

James knows a thing or two about food as well. He was head chef at The Star in Harome, one of the first pubs to win a Michelin star, and his menu pays great tribute to regional food and produce. You might find Harpham spring lamb with braised mutton and kidney faggots, Skipsea brill with cockle and crab stew, or ginger burnt cream with stewed Yorkshire rhubarb. There's plenty of game in season. James feels his main achievement has been sourcing good local produce and he is very proud of his suppliers, holding lunches and dinners at which the farmers and food producers get to meet his customers.

James is not bothered about Michelin recognition and has been adamant that The Pipe and Glass remains a pub as well as somewhere to come for something special. A list of pub grub classics runs alongside the main menu so if you don't want anything fancy you can have a rump steak sarnie with fried onions, Mapplethorpe sea-trout fish cakes, a dry-cure gammon steak with braised peas or 'a proper prawn cocktail'.

It's actually easier to run a little place than it is to make a successful dining pub of a venture of this size, with a big kitchen serving 1000 people a week. But James and Kate have managed it. They serve gaggles of ladies who lunch, sprawling family groups (the toddlers seated in beautiful, specially made wooden high chairs), walkers and locals. The Pipe and Glass pleases everyone.

the pipe and glass inn

WEST END, SOUTH DALTON, EAST YORKSHIRE, HU17 7PN • 01430 810246 • www.pipeandglass.co.uk
SERVES LUNCH (EXCEPT MONDAY) AND DINNER (EXCEPT SUNDAY AND MONDAY)

serves 4

4X 150G (5½OZ) PIECES OF WOOF
   FILLET, SKINNED

FOR THE MARINADE

200ML (7FL OZ) DRY WHITE WINE

200ML (7FL OZ) WHITE WINE VINEGAR

2 CARROTS, SLICED

2 CELERY STICKS, FINELY SLICED

2 SHALLOTS, FINELY SLICED

2TBSP GRATED FRESH GINGER

2 CHILLIES, HALVED, DESEEDED
   AND CHOPPED

1TSP FENNEL SEEDS

4 BAY LEAVES

SEA SALT AND PEPPER

1TBSP CASTER SUGAR

LEAVES FROM 1 BUNCH OF DILL, CHOPPED

FOR THE SALAD

500G (1LB 2OZ) JERUSALEM
   ARTICHOKES, CUBED

2TBSP FRESHLY GRATED HORSERADISH

1TBSP DIJON MUSTARD

SALT AND PEPPER

4TBSP MAYONNAISE

4TBSP CHOPPED CHIVES

soused scarborough woof with jerusalem artichoke & horseradish salad

Never heard of woof? Here is James's take on it: 'Scarborough woof is a type of catfish sometimes known as wolf fish. It's a frighteningly ugly fish and is grey with black spots, usually measuring about half a metre. The flesh has a firm texture and is bright white in appearance. It's mainly landed on the northeast coast and is not as costly as some other white fish. If you can't get it then use halibut or monkfish.'

Cut the fish into strips and lay around the inside of little ramekins (glass ones are particularly nice). Mix all the ingredients for the marinade together (except the dill) in a saucepan. Season to taste and simmer for 15 minutes. While the marinade is still hot, cover the fish with equal amounts of the marinade, including the vegetables and flavourings, then sprinkle the dill on top of each pot. Cover with clingfilm and chill in the fridge until required. They are better after 24 hours and will keep for up to 1 week.

For the salad, boil the artichokes in a little salted water until al dente. Drain and while still warm mix with the horseradish, mustard and salt and pepper, then add the mayonnaise and chives.

To serve, take the fish pots out of the fridge, remove the clingfilm and serve them with a spoonful of the artichoke salad on the plate and some toasted rye bread. This is also delicious served with pickled samphire.

GARLIC & CHILLI OLIVES £5.45

serves 4

4 BARNSLEY CHOPS	2TSP FINELY CHOPPED
SALT AND PEPPER	FLAT-LEAF PARSLEY
LEAVES FROM 2 SPRIGS FRESH THYME	1TSP GROUND CAYENNE PEPPER

FOR THE KIDNEYS

FOR THE SAUCE

4 LAMB'S KIDNEYS	4TBSP BLANCHED AND ROUGHLY
1TBSP VEGETABLE OIL	CHOPPED NETTLE LEAVES
GOOD DASH OF BRANDY	4TBSP ROUGHLY CHOPPED FRESH
200ML (7FL OZ) DOUBLE CREAM	MINT LEAVES
2TBSP STRONG ENGLISH MUSTARD	4TBSP WHITE WINE VINEGAR
4TBSP WHITE BREADCRUMBS	4TBSP OLIVE OIL
50G (1¾OZ) BUTTER	

grilled barnsley chop with devilled kidneys, nettle & mint sauce

A Barnsley chop is a double lamb chop. And don't be wary of cooking with nettles – give it a go. But make sure they're young ones.

Pick the nettles wearing gloves and keep them on to remove the leaves and discard the stalks. As soon as you blanch the leaves in boiling water they no longer sting.

Preheat the grill. Season the chops with salt, pepper and thyme and place on a greased metal baking sheet under a hot grill. Grill for about 10 minutes – 5 minutes on each side – or until done to your liking. Cover with foil, insulate and leave to rest.

Slice the kidneys in half and cut out the fatty sinew. Heat the oil in a frying pan and fry the kidneys for about 2 minutes on each side until golden brown and just cooked. Take the kidneys out of the pan and put them into a small ovenproof dish. Deglaze the pan with a little brandy then add the cream and mustard and reduce to a sauce consistency. Pour over the kidneys. Mix the crumbs, butter, parsley and cayenne together in a bowl and then sprinkle over the kidneys and grill until the crumbs are golden brown.

Place the nettles, mint, white wine vinegar and olive oil and some salt and pepper in a liquidizer and purée. Check the seasoning. To serve, place one chop on each plate with two half kidneys and spoon the nettle and mint sauce around. Serve with a caper and shallot salad and buttered new potatoes or crispy rosemary and garlic roast potatoes.

serves 4

2 OXTAILS, TRIMMED AND CUT INTO
  5–6CM (2INCH) PIECES
4 CARROTS
2 ONIONS
1 LEEK
4 CELERY STICKS
OLIVE OIL
PLAIN FLOUR
SALT AND PEPPER
1.2 LITRES (2PINTS) DARK BEER

1 LITRE (1¾PINTS) BEEF STOCK
2 BAY LEAVES
4 SPRIGS OF THYME
250G (9OZ) SELF-RAISING FLOUR
DASH OF WHITE WINE VINEGAR
4 FRESH SHUCKED OYSTERS
VEGETABLE OIL, FOR DEEP-FRYING
LEAVES OF SMALL BUNCH OF FLAT-
  LEAF PARSLEY, CHOPPED

beer-braised oxtails with oyster fritters

A good job James gave me the recipe for this: it's so melting and comforting (with the special touch of the oyster) that I would have to have stolen it otherwise. Buttery mash is the obvious and perfect accompaniment.

Trim any excess fat off the oxtail pieces and chop all the vegetables into even, medium-sized cubes. Heat 2tbsp olive oil in a large frying pan and fry the vegetables until golden brown. Remove from the pan and place in a bowl. Season some flour with salt and pepper and roll the oxtail pieces in it so they are just lightly coated.

Preheat the oven to 170°C/325°F/gas mark 3. Using the same pan as for the vegetables, sear the oxtails pieces until nice and brown. Do this in batches so that you don't have too many in the pan at once or else they won't brown properly. Put the browned oxtails into a deep ovenproof dish and cover with the browned vegetables. Deglaze the frying pan with 300ml (½pint) of the beer and strain over the oxtails. Add another 600ml (1pt) of beer, the beef stock, bay leaves and 3 of the sprigs of thyme. Season with pepper and a little salt. Cover with a tight-fitting lid or tin foil and place in the oven. Cook for 3–4 hours, or until the meat is very tender.

For the fritters, put the self-raising flour in a bowl with a little salt and pepper, the rest of the thyme leaves (chopped) and the white wine vinegar then whisk in the half pint of beer left over from before. Add enough cold water to make into a batter that coats the back of a spoon. Heat the oil to 180°C (350°F). Dip the oysters in a little flour and then dip them into the batter. Deep-fry until crispy and golden – it will only take about 40 seconds. Drain on kitchen paper. To serve, take the lid off the braised oxtails and sprinkle over the chopped parsley. Divide between bowls and spoon over the vegetables and cooking liquor. Place a hot crispy oyster on each one.

serves 4

FOR THE DAUPHINOISE

4 PARSNIPS

2 LARGE POTATOES, PEELED

500ML (18FL OZ) DOUBLE CREAM

2 CLOVES GARLIC, CRUSHED

150G (5½OZ) MATURE CHEDDAR
  CHEESE, GRATED

FOR THE DAMSONS

300G (10½OZ) DAMSONS

300ML (10FL OZ) PORT

3TBSP REDCURRANT JELLY

½ CINNAMON STICK

1TSP CRUSHED JUNIPER BERRIES

200ML (7FL OZ) RICH VEAL
  OR CHICKEN STOCK

LEMON JUICE (OPTIONAL)

4 OVEN-READY PARTRIDGES

4TBSP CHOPPED THYME

1TSP CRUSHED JUNIPER BERRIES

4 RASHERS STREAKY BACON

roast partridge with parsnip dauphinoise & mulled damsons

If you can get it, English grey-legged partridge is a real treat: plumper and slightly more flavoursome than the more common French red-legged. The dauphinoise and mulled damsons work well with other game too. If you can't get damsons, you can replace them with blackberries.

Preheat the oven to 180°C/350°F/gas mark 4. Slice the parsnip and potato very thinly, using a mandolin if you have one. Put the cream and garlic in a large saucepan and bring to the boil. Drop in the parsnip and potato and simmer for 5 minutes, making sure the potato and parsnip are mixed evenly. Season really well. Remove from the heat and place the parsnip and potato mixture in a buttered ovenproof dish and top with the grated cheese. Bake for about 40 minutes, or until the vegetables are completely tender.

Preheat the oven to 220°C/425°F/gas mark 7. Put the damsons into a bowl with a couple of tablespoons of water and cook in the microwave or in a saucepan until they are just tender enough to take the stones out. Place the partridges in a roasting tin and season with salt and pepper. Sprinkle over the thyme and the juniper. Place a rasher of bacon over the top of each bird. Roast for 15 minutes, then remove the bacon and cook the partridge for a further 10 minutes. Remove, cover with foil and then insulate with tea towels. Leave to rest while you make the sauce.

Deglaze the partridge roasting tin with the port then put the port into a saucepan with the redcurrant jelly and cinnamon. Reduce by half, add the stock and heat to boiling. Strain through a fine sieve into another saucepan and add the damsons. Heat together until tender. Taste and if necessary add more redcurrant jelly to sweeten or lemon juice to sharpen. To serve you can either remove the breast and legs from the partridge or serve it whole on the plate, with the bacon as garnish. Spoon the damsons and sauce over and serve with the dauphinoise on the side.

serves 4

FOR THE POSSET
500ML (18 FL OZ) DOUBLE CREAM
SMALL BUNCH OF LEMON VERBENA
125G (4½OZ) CASTER SUGAR
JUICE OF 2 LEMONS

FOR THE SPICED SUMMER BERRIES
175G (6OZ) EACH RASPBERRIES,
    BLACKBERRIES, REDCURRANTS AND
    STRAWBERRIES
300ML (10FL OZ) RED WINE

1 CINNAMON STICK
2 STAR ANISE
1 PINCH OF MIXED SPICE
200G (7OZ) CASTER SUGAR

FOR THE SUGAR CAKES
250G (9OZ) BUTTER, MELTED
125G (4½OZ) CASTER SUGAR
375G (13OZ) PLAIN FLOUR
1TSP GRATED NUTMEG
10 CLOVES, CRUSHED TO A POWDER

lemon verbena posset with spiced summer berries & east yorkshire sugar cakes

This can be made at any time of year – just leave out the lemon verbena, or substitute with a few sprigs of rosemary and replace the summer berries with autumn fruit such as blackberries, figs, pears and apples. The recipe for the sugar cakes is 300 years old and was found only last year by a Yorkshire historian. James was invited onto BBC Radio Humberside to cook them and liked them so much that they went on the menu that night.

Boil the cream with the lemon verbena (keep 4 sprigs back to garnish). When it comes up to boiling point add the sugar and lemon juice and stir until mixed. Pass through a sieve into a jug and then pour into serving glasses. Set in the fridge for at least 2 hours.

For the spiced fruit, hull the strawberries and halve the larger ones, and remove the currants from their stalks. Bring the red wine, cinnamon, star anise, mixed spice and sugar to the boil in a saucepan, stirring to help the sugar dissolve. Add the fruits, stir and remove from the heat. Leave the fruit to steep.

For the sugar cakes, preheat the oven to 170°C/325°F/gas mark 3. Mix all the ingredients together into a dough then roll into a thick sausage shape. Rest in the fridge for at least 30 minutes then cut into rounds 1cm (½inch) thick. Bake on a nonstick baking sheet for 10 minutes. Lift off and cool on a wire rack.

Spoon some of the fruit onto the top of each glass of lemon posset. Serve with the sugar cakes and sprigs of fresh lemon verbena.

serves 4

FOR THE PARKIN

200G (7OZ) GOLDEN SYRUP

50G (1¾OZ) BLACK TREACLE

200G (7OZ) SOFT DARK BROWN SUGAR

200G (7OZ) BUTTER

200G (7OZ) SELF-RAISING FLOUR

150G (5½OZ) ROLLED OATS

2 EGGS, BEATEN

4TSP GROUND GINGER

2TSP GROUND NUTMEG

2TSP GROUND MIXED SPICE

FOR THE CUSTARD

4 EGG YOLKS

65G (2¼OZ) CASTER SUGAR

25G (1OZ) PLAIN FLOUR

250ML (9FL OZ) MILK

½ VANILLA POD, SPLIT

1 KNOB OF FRESH ROOT GINGER, PEELED
  AND GRATED

FOR THE CHANTILLY CREAM

500ML (18FL OZ) DOUBLE CREAM

½ VANILLA POD, SPLIT

1TBSP TOASTED FLAKED ALMONDS

50G (1¾OZ) ICING SUGAR, PLUS EXTRA
  FOR DUSTING

8 STICKS OF FORCED PINK RHUBARB

CASTER SUGAR, TO TASTE

4–6 DROPS GRENADINE

RUM, TO TASTE

forced yorkshire rhubarb trifle with rum-soaked parkin crumbs

You can used bought ginger cake but parkin is a traditional Yorkshire cake and is very easy to make.

To make the parkin, preheat the oven to 170°C/325°F/gas mark 3. Heat the syrup, treacle, sugar and butter in a large saucepan. Stir in the flour, oats, eggs and spices. Pour into a greased Swiss roll tin lined with nonstick baking paper, and bake for 10–12 minutes. Remove from oven and cool in the tin. Turn the oven up to 180°C/ 350°F/gas mark 4. Cut the rhubarb into 5cm (2 inch) pieces and put in a baking dish with 100ml of water over and caster sugar, to taste, and the grenadine. Cover with tin foil and bake for 10–15 minutes, or until just poached. Leave the rhubarb to cool, then pour the liquor into a saucepan and reduce to a syrup by boiling. Cool.

To make the custard, whisk the egg yolks and sugar, then add the flour and whisk until well combined. Bring the milk to the boil with the vanilla and ginger and then strain over the egg mixture, stirring all the time (discard the ginger). Whisk and return to the pan. Cook and thicken over a moderate heat for about 5 minutes, constantly stirring. Pour into a bowl and cover with clingfilm to prevent a skin forming. Leave to cool and put in the fridge. Whip the double cream with the icing sugar and the scraped-out seeds of the vanilla pod. You should have soft peaks. Fold one-third of the whipped Chantilly cream through the custard. To make the trifles, crumble some parkin into the bottom of 4 glasses or a bowl and pour on some rum. Spoon in some of the poached rhubarb followed by custard, then some cream on top. Finish with the rhubarb syrup (use enough to make it pretty but don't drown the trifle), toasted almonds and a dusting of icing sugar.

the best of the rest

the blackwell ox inn

The food is the thing here. Chef-patron Steve Holding loves the rustic, bold cooking of Spain and south-west France and it's great to find this sun-drenched, gutsy food so far from its home. You can enjoy cassoulet or salt cod fritters with aïoli and smoked paprika as well as traditional British dishes (apple crumble and custard, and fish and chips) and more refined offerings using great Yorkshire produce, such as Ribblesdale blue goats' cheese tart with poached pears and local honey. Eat in the lovely bar, with its bottle-green walls and wooden floor, or the rather formal dining room.
Huby Road, Sutton-on-the-Forest, North Yorkshire, YO61 1DT, Tel. 01347 810328, www.blackwelloxinn.co.uk Serves lunch and dinner every day, rooms available.

the blue lion

This must be one of the most gorgeous places in the book (reviewers have more than once described it as one of the loveliest places to eat in England) because of its authentic open interior. With its big high ceilings, tongue and groove and stone floors you feel that you are going back in time as you enter. And then there's the menu which is a riot of earthy, appetite-inducing dishes: blue Wensleydale tart with tomato chutney, beef suet pudding with dark onion gravy, creamy gratin of smoked haddock, egg, leeks and mushrooms. Dream pub food.
East Witton, Leyburn, North Yorkshire, DL8 4SN Tel. 01969 624273, www.thebluelion.co.uk Serves lunch and dinner every day, rooms available.

the fleece

Oh to end up here on a cold, rainy day…low ceilings, blazing fires, dark cosy corners, real ales on tap and a warm Yorkshire welcome. Bliss. The menu is huge. And it's all good, local north-country stuff: Whitby haddock with chips, a very piggy-tasting honey and mustard roast belly of pork, braised Wharfedale lamb. This is gutsy, quintessentially pub food and there aren't many concessions to modern, metropolitan tastes. Portions are huge. Absolutely cracking.
Main Street, Addingham, Ilkley, West Yorkshire, LS29 0LY Tel. 01943 830491. Serves lunch and dinner every day (until 8:15pm on Sunday).

the golden lion

I passed this by when I researched my first book on dining pubs as the food was inconsistent and the place lacked atmosphere but a change of ownership has pulled The Golden Lion round. There aren't any fireworks; the food is decidedly simple – mussels in white wine, fish cakes with sorrel sauce, steak and kidney pudding – and some of it is quite retro (a rich and boozy pork stroganoff) But it's all done very well. A lack of heavy furnishings and pub paraphernalia – there's just simple dark wood furniture, white walls and lots of candles – make it feel contemporary.
6 West End, Osmotherley, North Yorkshire, DL6 3AA Tel. 01609 883526, www.goldenlionosmotherley.co.uk Serves lunch and dinner every day.

kaye arms

This is the kind of old-fashioned dining pub that was thriving way before anyone ever thought of gastropubs as a concept – it's a no-nonsense, honest, traditional place – though that doesn't mean the cooking is out of date. You'll find contemporary dishes such as sea bass with provençal vegetables alongside modern pub classics such as roast pork belly with mustard mash. Puddings are nursery-like and the staff are salt of the earth. The place is absolutely thronged at the weekend – locals love the place – so be sure to book.
29 Wakefield Road, Grange Moor, West Yorkshire, WF4 4BG Tel. 01924 848385. Serves lunch and dinner (except Monday).

the oak tree inn

This is the kind of pub I love to find. On the face of it it's just a little cottage at the end of a terrace but Alastair and Claire Ross have created a very special place. Alastair, who has cooked at the Savoy and Leith's, offers a good mixture of contemporary and old-fashioned dishes: you might find roast lamb with pommes dauphinoises, sea bream with crab cannelloni and shellfish sauce, and wine poached plums with honey and yoghurt ice-cream. The dark green dining room is charming – oak tables, white cloths and pews – and there are bunches of flowers everywhere. A little gem.
Hutton Magna, Richmond, North Yorkshire, DL11 7HH Tel. 01833 627371, www.elevation-it.co.uk/oaktree Serves lunch and dinner (except Monday).

the old bore

An eccentric and rather wonderful place, so stuffed with quirky antiques (mirrors, antlers, and old prints), it's difficult to know where to focus (kids will love it). Maverick owner and chef Scott Hessel has cooked in such illustrious places as La Tante Claire in London but fanciness is not in evidence here. The food is exactly what you want to eat in a pub – prawn cocktail with a whiskey-laced sauce, smoked duck breast with beer pickled onions, pheasant with suet pudding, and Whitby cod with chips and mushy peas. Lovely special touches too, such as homemade flavoured gins and vodkas.

Oldham Road, Rishworth, Halifax, West Yorkshire, HX6 4QU, Tel. 01422 822291, www.oldbore.co.uk. Serves lunch and dinner (except Monday and Tuesday).

the sandpiper inn

Generally I go for the bar rather than the dining room but here the dining room – a lovely, calming space with soft green painted walls and dark wooden tables – is the place to be. The bar, with its pine furniture, has much less character, though locals and those clamouring for space don't seem to mind. Chef Jonathan Harrison produces food from all over the globe – Moroccan chicken, beef in Guinness, poached salmon with fennel and garlic mayonnaise – together with pub stalwarts such as fishcakes and rib eye steaks. Puds are the usual suspects – sticky toffee pudding and crème brulée.

Market Place, Leyburn, North Yorkshire, DL8 5AT Tel. 01969 622206, www.sandpiperinn.co.uk Serves lunch and dinner (except Monday), rooms available.

shibden mill inn

The food here is good rather than great, but as a whole this is a lovely, relaxing place made up of a real warren of rooms where you can just lose yourself. The dining room (with smart napery, pristine glassware et al.) offers ambitious cooking, but go for the bar and its simpler food. There they do good versions of pub classics – steak, fish pie, cottage pie and burgers – and there's even a knickerbocker glory on the dessert menu. The staff are unstuffy and friendly, and the setting – beside a bubbling brook – is blissful.

Shibden, Halifax, West Yorkshire HX3 7UL Tel. 01422 365840, www.shibdenmillinn.com Serves lunch and dinner every day, rooms available.

the travellers rest

An old stone pub on the Yorkshire moors with staggering views, this is the place to come to get away from it all. Everything is resolutely traditional – flagstone floors, big fires, exposed stone, old beams – softened with lovely fabrics and lighting. Food is old-fashioned – smoked salmon roulade, pork with mustard sauce, lamb with red currant gravy – and good, and is served in both the bar and the dining room (the bar menu also has more pubby offerings such as steak and ale pie and jam roly poly). Locals love it and it's become a bit of a destination dining place, too.

Steep Lane, Sowerby, Halifax, West Yorkshire, HX6 1PE Tel. 01422 832124, www.travellersrestsowerby.co.uk Serves lunch and dinner (except Monday and Tuesday).

the wensleydale heifer inn

This handsome, 17th-century whitewashed coaching inn fits into the 'smart pub' category – roaring fire, tartan carpets and gorgeous leather sofas in the lounge, a dining room with napery and the bistro-like 'Fish Bar'. The food is great, particularly the fish (despite the fact that West Witton is miles from the sea). Knowingly naff touches – pictures of seafaring cows and maritime paraphernalia – don't lead you to expect the high level of cooking delivered. Whitby cod in a batter made from Black Sheep Bitter, fat chips and mushy peas could hardly be bettered.

Main Street, West Witton, North Yorkshire, DL8 4LS Tel. 01969 622322, www.wensleydaleheifer.co.uk Serves lunch and dinner every day, rooms available.

the white swan inn

The White Swan is more hotel than pub, but it has a great bar with deep red walls, a huge log fire and well-kept Yorkshire ales plus no-nonsense delicious food, all sourced as locally as possible. The famed Ginger Pig is nearby and supplies the pub with all its meat and poultry. The dining room is a handsome flagstoned affair where you can feast on grilled white pudding with smoked bacon and wild mushrooms, chargrilled rib eye of Longhorn beef with proper homemade chips, or toasted Ginger Pig ham and Fountains Gold cheese sandwich. The bread, ice-cream, chutneys and even the ketchup are all homemade.

Market Place, Pickering, North Yorkshire, YO18 7AA Tel. 01751 472288, www.white-swan.co.uk Serves lunch and dinner every day, rooms available.

scotland

It may stand on a street corner in the dockyard area of Leith but as soon as you enter The King's Wark you think you're in Spain. The smell of chorizo, garlic, warm olive oil and fresh fish fills your nostrils, and you might glimpse a flash of fire as booze is added to a pan in the kitchen. Then you look at the specials board (which changes daily) and you wonder whether you are in Edinburgh or Barcelona: chunky fish stew with smoked paprika mayonnaise, lamb with capers and olive oil mash, and seared scallops with roast peppers sit alongside the redoubtably Scottish venison with berry and port sauce and cranachan with shortbread.

Chef Michael Greig is an Edinburgh man but his mum is from Gibraltar and his grandmother from Spain, so he grew up with the flavours of Iberia. 'Oh I was picked on in school because I smelt of garlic,' he says. 'That was unusual in Edinburgh when I was a boy. We ate squid, prawns and mussels at home, not just mince and tatties.'

Michael's heroes are Hugh Fearnley-Whittingstall and the fearlessly offal-focused chef, Fergus Henderson. He likes solid, homely, peasant food, though his dishes are delivered with the degree of polish you expect from a chef, not just a good home cook. He feels that his cooking is 'in continuous development' otherwise he would get bored. It's not unusual for Michael to think of a dish during service, make it and add it to the specials board.

For a long time he focused on fish but these days he is pretty obsessed by pigs and is always trying new dishes and unfamiliar cuts of pork. He has also been smitten by the trend for using every bit of an animal. 'It's partly because chefs have to be thrifty,' he says. 'But also because you want to avoid waste – from an ethical point of view – and to enjoy the sheer pleasure of trying to find uses for a particular ingredient or off-cut. In the pub I can be a bit left of field in what I try out. Regulars especially are really up for trying new dishes.'

The pub's manager (and Michael's partner) Lesley Currie has been at The King's Wark for nigh on 10 years and her presence – you get a terrifically warm welcome – is as important as the food. They make a great team. And as if this wasn't enough, The King's Wark is one of the most characterful pubs in this book. It's one of the oldest buildings in Leith. There are bare stone walls, stained by the smoke from the log fire, aged anaglypta wallpaper, a wild mural on the ceiling, absolutely gleaming beer pumps and dripping candles set in old bottles on every table. Edinburgh has plenty of good high-end restaurants and characterful drinking pubs but it really needed a great dining pub.
Its denizens must be thrilled with The King's Wark.

the king's wark

36 THE SHORE, EDINBURGH, EH6 6QU • TEL 0131 554 9260
SERVES LUNCH AND DINNER EVERY DAY

serves 6

2 PIG'S TROTTERS

75ML (2FL OZ) SHERRY

2 X 340G (12OZ) CAN DUCK OR
  GOOSE FAT

4 SADDLES OF RABBIT

75G (3OZ) BUTTER

2 LARGE LEEKS, VERY FINELY SLICED

150G (5½OZ) BUTTER, MELTED

SALT AND PEPPER

FOR THE STOCK

2 CARROTS

2 CELERY STICKS

1 ONION, HALVED

1 LEEK, ROUGHLY CHOPPED

2 BAY LEAVES

2 BLACK PEPPERCORNS

FOR THE CHUTNEY

8 STALKS RHUBARB, THINLY SLICED

2 THINLY SLICED RED ONIONS

1 RED CHILLI, DESEEDED AND FINELY
  DICED

2CM (¾ INCH) SQUARE FRESH ROOT
  GINGER, PEELED AND FINELY CHOPPED

125ML (4FL OZ) CIDER VINEGAR

250G (8OZ) CASTER SUGAR

pork & rabbit rillettes with rhubarb & ginger chutney

Serve a generous scoop of rillettes with the chutney and some toasted bread.

Preheat the oven to 180°C/350°C/gas mark 4. Cover the pig's trotters with water, bring to the boil and cook for 10 minutes, skimming off the scum, then remove, wipe and put in an ovenproof pan. Cover with water and add all the stock ingredients. Bring to the boil. Cover, transfer to the oven and cook for 2½ hours or until the trotters are tender. Lift them out and set aside. Strain the stock, add the sherry and boil to reduce by about three-quarters. The liquid should look quite syrupy. When the trotters are cool enough to handle, pull the meat off the bones and shred.

Gently melt the duck or goose fat in a saucepan in which the rabbit can sit really snugly. When the fat is liquid add the rabbit saddles (the fat should cover them) and cook on the stovetop over a very gentle heat for 2 hours, or until the meat is very tender. Remove the saddles and leave until just cool enough to handle. Take the meat off the bones and shred. Melt the butter in a pan and gently sauté the leeks until soft, stirring occasionally. The leeks should be completely soft but not coloured. In a large bowl, mix all the rabbit and trotter meat, the cooked leeks, reduced stock and melted butter. The mixture shouldn't be too runny so add the stock carefully (you may not need it all). Season very well. Line a loaf tin – 13x23x7cm (5x9x3inch) – with clingfilm and put the mixture into it, pressing it down well. Cover and place in the fridge overnight. (If you want to serve the rillettes in individual portions then pack them into little ramekin dishes instead.)

Cook the rhubarb for 3 minutes in 2tbsp water then add the red onion, chilli and ginger and cook for further 3 minutes. Add the vinegar and sugar. Bring gently to the boil, stirring to help the sugar dissolve, then turn the heat down. Cover and leave to simmer, checking it does not catch and burn, for 30 minutes. Cool and store till you want to use it.

serves 4

2 DRESSED CRABS
CRACKED BLACK PEPPER
PINCH CAYENNE PEPPER
GOOD SQUEEZE OF LEMON JUICE
200G (7OZ) BABY SPINACH LEAVES

4 QUAIL'S EGGS
4 CHERRY VINE TOMATOES, HALVED
4 ANCHOVY FILLETS, HALVED
100G (3½OZ) BUTTER, MELTED

potted crab with anchovies & soft-boiled quail's eggs

The notion of a classic 'with a twist' is not usually one that appeals – it generally means the spirit of a perfectly good dish has been ruined by pointless tampering. But this is simple and good: potted crab with knobs on.

Separate the brown and white crab meat and season each type with cracked black pepper, a pinch of cayenne pepper and a squeeze of lemon juice.

Blanch the spinach leaves quickly in boiling water and immediately plunge into iced water. Lift them out and dry really well but don't squeeze the spinach in your fists as you do for many Italian recipes.

Boil the quail's eggs for 45 seconds, leave in the water for another 45 seconds and then plunge into cold water. Peel off the shell. Place a layer of spinach in each of 4 glasses, then top each with half a quail's egg, half a tomato and half an anchovy. Repeat these layers, then press the brown meat into the glasses and put the white meat on top. Divide the melted butter between the four glasses and allow to set in the fridge. Remove them 10–15 minutes before serving. Offer toasted bread on the side.

serves 4

2 SMALL MORCILLA SAUSAGES
2 SMALL CHORIZO SAUSAGES
900G (2LB) WAXY POTATOES
4 X 175G (6OZ) HAKE FILLETS
50G (1¾OZ) PLAIN FLOUR
SALT AND PEPPER
1 TBSP SMOKED PAPRIKA
OLIVE OIL, FOR FRYING
500G (1LB 2OZ) PURPLE SPROUTING
  OR TENDERSTEM BROCCOLI
200G (7OZ) FINE GREEN BEANS

FOR THE GREEN SAUCE
LEAVES FROM SMALL BUNCH OF
  CURLY PARSLEY
LEAVES FROM SMALL BUNCH OF
  FLAT-LEAF PARSLEY
1 TSP FRESH THYME LEAVES
1 CLOVE GARLIC, CRUSHED
1 TBSP CAPERS, RINSED OF SALT OR BRINE
JUICE OF 1 LEMON
1 MEDIUM RED OR GREEN CHILLI,
  DESEEDED AND CHOPPED
250ML (9FL OZ) EXTRA VIRGIN OLIVE OIL

hake, morcilla & chorizo with potatoes & salsa verde

This dish shows Michael's Spanish roots. Fish and pork is a classic Iberian combination.

To make the green sauce, blitz all the ingredients, except the olive oil, in a food processor. With the food processor going, steadily trickle in the oil until you have a mixture slightly thinner than mayonnaise. Check for seasoning, cover and keep in the fridge until needed (bringing it out of the fridge shortly before serving).

Slice the morcilla and the chorizo into 1.5 cm (½ inch) thick slices. Boil the potatoes until tender and keep warm. Lightly dust the hake fillets in flour seasoned with salt, pepper and smoked paprika. Heat 2tbsp olive oil in a frying pan. Place the fillets skin-side down and cook over a medium heat for 3 minutes, until the skin is nicely browned, then turn the fillets over and cook for a further 3 minutes on the other side.

While you are doing this, steam or boil the broccoli and the green beans until they are cooked but still have a little bite. Drain. Heat 2tbsp olive oil in another frying pan and cook the chorizo and morcilla until coloured on both sides and cooked through.

Divide the potatoes, greens, chorizo and morcilla between 4 plates, drizzling with the oil from the pan in which you cooked the sausages. Top with a dollop of salsa verde and then put the hake on top, skin-side up.

serves 6

4 BRAMLEY APPLES, PEELED, CORED
   AND CHOPPED
2 STALKS RHUBARB, CHOPPED
500G (1LB 2OZ) GOOSEBERRIES,
   TRIMMED
50G (1¾OZ) UNSALTED BUTTER
75G (2½OZ) SOFT BROWN SUGAR
JUICE AND RIND OF 1 LEMON

FOR THE COBBLER TOPPING
225G (8OZ) SELF-RAISING FLOUR
100G (3½OZ) UNSALTED BUTTER
50G (2OZ) CASTER SUGAR

GRATED RIND OF 1 LEMON
1 EGG, BEATEN
50ML (2FL OZ) FULL-FAT MILK
1 EGG, BEATEN, FOR GLAZING
BROWN SUGAR

FOR THE ICE-CREAM
2TBSP HEATHER HONEY
45ML (2FL OZ) LAPHROAIG MALT
   WHISKY (OR ANY PEATY WHISKY)
3 LARGE EGGS, SEPARATED
150G (5½OZ) CASTER SUGAR
450ML (16FL OZ) DOUBLE CREAM

apple, rhubarb & gooseberry cobbler with heather honey & laphroaig whisky ice-cream

I love the way this cobbler includes three different fruits. When gooseberries aren't in season you could increase the quantity of the rhubarb and apples and still make the dish. And this glorious ice-cream doesn't even need churning. If you don't want to use Laophraig, you can use any other whisky, but Michael likes the way its slightly peaty flavour comes through
in the ice.

To make the ice-cream, heat the honey and whisky together until blended, then leave to cool. Using an electric mixer, whisk the egg yolks with the sugar and the honey mixture until pale. Whisk the cream to soft peaks, then in another bowl (and using a clean whisk or beaters) beat the egg whites until they form medium peaks. Fold half of the cream into the beaten yolk mix, followed by half of the egg white. Repeat until everything is mixed together. Put this into a shallow plastic container and freeze overnight.

For the cobbler topping, sift the flour into a bowl then rub in the butter until the mixture resembles breadcrumbs. Mix in the sugar, grated lemon rind and egg, then add the milk. Mix until everything comes together into a ball. Cover with clingfilm and put in the fridge.

Preheat the oven to 190°C/375°F/gas mark 5. On a low heat, cook the fruit until soft in a pan with the butter, sugar and lemon juice and rind over a low heat until soft. Put into a baking dish. Roll out the dough 1cm (⅓ inch) thick and cut into 2cm (⅔ inch) rounds with a cookie cutter. Put the rounds onto the mixture in the baking dish, glaze with egg and sprinkle with brown sugar. Bake for 30 minutes or until golden.

serves 4

450G (1LB) MIXED BERRIES (SUCH AS
   STRAWBERRIES, RASPBERRIES, TAYBERRIES,
   LOGANBERRIES, BLACKBERRIES, AND RED, BLACK
   AND WHITE CURRANTS)

FOR THE SYRUP

JUICE OF 2 LEMONS
4 STAR ANISE
75ML (2½FL OZ) CRABBIES GREEN GINGER WINE
75ML (2½FL OZ) WATER
1 VANILLA POD, SPLIT

summer berries with crabbies, ginger wine & star anise syrup

At The King's Wark they use whatever mixture of berries is around, though I prefer the softer berries to strawberries. The syrup also goes very well with lightly poached stone fruit.

Put all the ingredients for the syrup into a pan and heat gently, stirring to help the sugar dissolve. Bring to the boil and reduce until the liquid mixture has a syrupy texture. Remove the vanilla pod. Leave to cool completely.

Prepare the berries – all you need to do is hull the strawberries and halve or quarter any very large ones – and remove the stalks from any of the berries which have them. Put into a large bowl, or individual bowls, and pour over the syrup. Serve with ice-cream.

'It may stand on a street corner in the dockyard area of Leith but as soon as you enter The King's Wark you think you're in Spain. The smell of chorizo, garlic, warm olive oil and fresh fish fills your nostrils.'

It does your heart good to arrive here at twilight, the air damp with dricht and smelling of chimney smoke, and read a menu that is full of Scottish ingredients, enthusiasm and intelligence. I have met many chef-proprietors in Scotland at a loss to explain why the country's best produce leaves on articulated lorries bound for France and Spain, so it's a thrill to see Scrabster scallops, Finnan haddock and venison from Aberfoyle all listed here. And the Scottish dishes offered by chefs James Fletcher and Laurie Veitch are no sentimental homage to a faux Scottish culinary tradition. The haggis fritters, which could be a disaster in less capable hands, are made with Cockburn's superb haggis, and served with the inn's apple chutney and are spicy, melt-in-the-mouth wonderful.

Laurie and James are both self-taught cooks. James's parents had a restaurant in Somerset so he grew up in the business and started waiting at tables when he was just 10 years old. Laurie is a local whose home life revolved around the great food cooked by her mum. They met when James was studying at Stirling University and Laurie was working at a restaurant in the city. The couple exhibit that raw excitement which the best self-taught chefs have: they are constantly learning and trying out new dishes and are not hidebound by rules or the strictures of a classical training. Cookery books lie open and splattered around the kitchen and tomes by Claudia Roden and Sam and Sam Clark of Moro are full of yellow stickers marking pages of interest. There might be huge vats of chickpeas and beans soaking in water as part of the preparations for an evening of Moroccan food. James and Laurie are doing what it is possible to do in a pub: offering dishes that are essentially home food, but in an elevated version.

The Inn at Kippen made me want to weep, though. This roadside pub is in a pretty Scottish village, not too far from Glasgow and Edinburgh. The couple source impeccably – the game is from a dealer in Auchterarder, fish is never on the menu before Thursday (that's when they believe the best stuff comes in), smoked salmon comes from nearby Nick Nairn and the Salar smokehouse on the Isle of Uist, and their salad leaves were the best I tasted while researching this book – and take risks such as building a wood-fired pizza oven outside (which is on the go every weekend, even when it's lashing down). The menu is great. The place looks cosy, welcoming and well-kept. Yet the Inn at Kippen is half-empty on weekday lunchtimes.

Denizens of Stirlingshire, Glasgow and Edinburgh, and holiday makers touring these parts, get yourselves to Kippen! Or the Inn will disappear – and the Scottish food map will be that much poorer without it.

the inn at kippen

FORE ROAD, KIPPEN, STIRLINGSHIRE, FK8 3DT • TEL 01786 871010 • www.theinnatkippen.co.uk
SERVES LUNCH AND DINNER EVERY DAY

serves 4

16 LARGE SCALLOPS
GROUNDNUT OIL
SALT AND PEPPER

FOR THE SWEET CHILLI SAUCE
6 LARGE FRESH RED CHILLIES,
 ROUGHLY CHOPPED
5CM (2INCH) SQUARE PIECE OF
 FRESH ROOT GINGER, PEELED AND
 ROUGHLY CHOPPED
3 LEMON GRASS STALKS,
 ROUGHLY CHOPPED
10 FRESH LIME LEAVES
GRATED RIND OF 3 LIMES
12 CLOVES GARLIC, PEELED

LARGE BUNCH OF CORIANDER LEAVES
300G (10½OZ) CASTER SUGAR
50ML (2FL OZ) THAI FISH SAUCE
120ML (4FL OZ) WHITE WINE VINEGAR

FOR THE ORIENTAL SALAD
1 SMALL CARROT
4 SPRING ONIONS
1 RED PEPPER, HALVED AND DESEEDED
200G (7OZ) MIZUNA LEAVES, OR
 WATERCRESS OR LAMB'S LETTUCE IF
 YOU CAN'T GET MIZUNA
50G (1¾OZ) BEAN SPROUTS
HANDFUL OF CORIANDER LEAVES

scallops with sweet chilli sauce & oriental salad

At the Inn they use the biggest diver-caught scallops from Scrabster to make this dish, but obviously any good fat scallops will do. The salad also works well with big prawns. The sauce recipe makes much more than you need but it's one of those things you might as well make in quantity if you are going to make it at all, and it keeps well in the fridge in a screw-top jar.

Put the chillies, ginger, lemon grass, lime leaves, lime rind, garlic and coriander leaves into a food processor and purée into a coarse paste. Put the sugar into a heavy-based pan with 6tbsp water and place on a medium heat until the sugar dissolves. Turn the heat up gradually and gently boil until the syrup turns to a caramel colour. Stir in the spice paste, fish sauce and vinegar and simmer for 2 minutes.

For the salad, cut the carrot into long thin strips and the spring onions into long shreds. Cut the pepper into long thin shreds as well. Mix all this with the leaves, bean sprouts and coriander.

To serve, lightly oil the scallops and season with salt and pepper. Heat a frying pan until very hot and sear the scallops for 1 minute on each side. The scallops should be just cooked on the inside. Divide the salad between the plates. Set the scallops on top of the salad and drizzle with some of the sweet chilli sauce.

'It does your heart good to arrive here at twilight, the damp air smelling of chimney smoke, and read a menu that is full of Scottish ingredients, enthusiasm and intelligence.'

serves 10

FOR THE APPLE CHUTNEY

1½ TBSP SUNFLOWER OIL

300G (10½OZ) SHALLOTS, QUARTERED
OR HALVED IF LARGE, SMALL ONES
LEFT WHOLE

1 GREEN CHILLI, FINELY CHOPPED

5CM (2INCH) SQUARE PIECE OF FRESH
ROOT GINGER, PEELED AND GRATED

4 CLOVES GARLIC, CRUSHED

1KG (2LB 4OZ) BRAMLEY APPLES,
PEELED, CORED AND DICED

250G (9OZ) SULTANAS

4TSP CINNAMON

6 CLOVES, CRUSHED

6 CARDAMOM PODS, CRUSHED

2TSP GROUND CORIANDER

1TSP GROUND CUMIN

450ML (16FL OZ) CIDER VINEGAR

700G (1LB 9OZ) CASTER SUGAR

FOR THE BEER BATTER

175G (6OZ) SELF-RAISING FLOUR

175G (6OZ) CORNFLOUR

PINCH OF SALT

600ML (1PINT) LAGER

100ML (3½FL OZ) SODA WATER

750G (1½LB) BLACK PUDDING

BEEF DRIPPING, FOR DEEP-FRYING

PLAIN FLOUR, FOR DIPPING

DRESSED SALAD LEAVES, TO SERVE

black pudding fritters with apple chutney

This is the kind of dish that could go badly wrong but they do a great job of it
at the Inn at Kippen, where they also make it with haggis.

To make the chutney, heat the oil in a large saucepan or preserving pan. Sauté the shallots, chilli,
ginger and garlic over a medium heat for 10 minutes. Add all the remaining ingredients to the
pan and simmer for approximately 1 hour, stirring every 10 minutes to prevent the chutney from
sticking. When the chutney is ready, spoon into sterilized jars and seal while still hot. Leave to
cool and then store in the fridge for a week before using.

To make the beer batter, sift together the flours and salt. Whisk in the lager and soda water.
To make the fritters, cut the black pudding into medallions roughly 1cm/½ inch thick. Heat the
dripping to 170°C/325°F. Dip the black pudding pieces into plain flour then into the beer batter.
Deep-fry the fritters for 2–3 minutes until they are golden. Meanwhile, gently heat the chutney.

Remove the black pudding fritters from the fryer and place on kitchen paper to drain away
the excess oil. Place a small amount of chutney on each plate and put the haggis fritters on top.
Serve with dressed leaves.

leek, shallot & parmesan tartlets

This was my favourite dish at Kippen: light and savoury and absolutely melting. And it's terrifically easy to make.

Serves 6

FOR THE SHALLOT CONFIT
125G (4½OZ) BUTTER
450G (1LB) SHALLOTS, PEELED AND FINELY SLICED
100G (3½ OZ) CASTER SUGAR
125ML (4FL OZ) RED WINE VINEGAR
50ML (2FL OZ) SHERRY VINEGAR
LEAVES FROM 4 SPRIGS OF FRESH THYME

FOR THE TARTLETS
350G (11½OZ) PUFF PASTRY
400G (14OZ) LEEKS, FINELY CHOPPED
250G (9OZ) FRESHLY GRATED PARMESAN
3 EGGS
280ML (½PINT) DOUBLE CREAM
50ML (2FL OZ) CRÈME FRAÎCHE
A GOOD GRATING OF NUTMEG
SALT AND PEPPER
DRESSED LEAVES, TO SERVE

Melt the butter and sauté the shallots in it over a low heat until very soft. Add the sugar, vinegars and thyme leaves. Simmer for about 1 hour over a low heat until all the liquid has reduced to a thick syrup. Preheat the oven to 180°C/350F/Gas 4. Roll the pastry on a lightly floured surface and use it to line six individual tartlet tins measuring 10cm (4 inches) across. Line these with greaseproof paper, add baking beans and bake blind for 7 minutes. Remove the paper and beans and bake for a further 4 minutes until crisp. Mix everything for the tart filling together along with the shallot confit and stir well. Fill the tart cases then bake for 10–12 minutes or until the mixture is set. Leave to cool a little, slip out of the tart tins and serve with dressed leaves.

elizabeth's tablet

Scottish fudge, tablet, is a little firmer than regular fudge. At Kippen they serve this with coffee. You can add vanilla extract if you like and other flavours – coffee, whisky, rum and raisin – work well too.

makes 1 trayful
925G (2LB 1OZ) GRANULATED SUGAR
100G (3½OZ) BUTTER
250ML (9FL OZ) MILK
200G (7OZ) CAN CONDENSED MILK

Mix all the ingredients in a large pan, stirring well. Slowly heat, stirring occasionally to help dissolve the sugar and melt the butter. Increase the temperature and bring the mixture to the boil. Reduce the heat but keep the surface of the mixture gently bubbling for approximately 20 minutes, stirring as often as you can. This stage requires careful attention to prevent the mixture boiling or burning on the bottom of the pan.

After 20 minutes are up, the mixture should have thickened and be a pale coffee colour. Remove from the heat. Beat with a hand-held electric whisk, or vigorously with a wooden spoon, for approximately 5 minutes (10 minutes if it is by hand). Do this carefully as the mixture will still be hot. Beating ensures the formation of very small crystals while the mixture is cooling. You want to get it to the 'soft ball' stage. (Drop a little of the mixture into a glass of water to test – if it forms a soft gall it is ready). If you feel the mixture becoming 'grainy', stop beating at once – it is ready.

Line a 23 x 33cm (9 x 14inch) Swiss roll tin with nonstick baking paper and pour in the mixture, then leave to set. Once the tablet is firmish, cut it into squares while it is still in the tin, then leave to set completely overnight.

index

acknowledgements

So many people worked hard on this book that I feel bad about having only my name on the cover. All the chefs who feature gave up time to talk to me and then tested and wrote up the recipes you find in here (and chefs hate testing and writing). My whole-hearted thanks to them. They have made it a joy.

The biggest thanks goes to my editor Hattie Ellis and designer Miranda Harvey. They put in more effort, passion and care than their jobs require. Simon Wheeler went off around the country taking his pictures with the minimum of fuss and very little input from me. He is one of the few photographers who can do everything – landscapes, portraits and food – and he has come up trumps. Thanks to commissioning editor Rebecca Spry who was as supportive, constructive and sharp as ever. And to Mitchell Beazley for liking my ideas and backing them.

Loads of people ferried me around the country on mad gastropub eating jaunts – and that's not always as fun as it sounds – or were willing dining companions, so a big thank you to Aliza O'Keefe, Bruce and Olive Thompson, Anne Booth-Clibborn, Lucy Bannell, Matt Tebbutt, Mark Taylor, Fiona Smith, Janice Gabriel, Anne Kennedy, Hattie and Becca (again) my sister, Lesley, and my mum and dad. Mark Taylor did a good job of alerting me to new places and was endlessly generous with his time and advice. Stephen Harris – from The Sportsman in Seasalter in Kent – was always a great person to chew the fat with about pubs and food.

Finally thanks to Pete and Vicky at The Hardwick for making Stephen Terry write up his recipes even when he was in the middle of filming for The Great British Menu, and a warm hug and limitless gratitude to Mari Smit who keeps my life from being totally chaotic.